ATLANTIC COAST LINE

Standard Railroad of the South

by
William E. Griffin, Jr.

2001
TLC PUBLISHING INC.
1387 WINDING CREEK LANE
LYNCHBURG, VA 24503-3776

The first of the R-1's, No. 1800, poses for the ACL's company photographer at Waycross, Georgia. *(ACL Photo)*

Cover Photo

The Atlantic Coast Line's distinctive purple, gold and silver paint scheme was recreated here from a original black and white photograph by designer Ken Miller. The nose herald is the only part that is different from real life, as it was only purple on a stainless plate.

End Sheets

Front: IC E7-A No. 4009, having run through from Chicago with the *City of Miami*, joins the lineup of ACL E6-A Nos. 512, 516, 509 and 503 at the Jacksonville roundhouse on July 30, 1947. *(ACL Photo)*

Rear: R-1 Class 4-8-4 No. 1805 was photographed during a station stop at Charleston, South Carolina with the *Havana Special's* train of heavyweight equipment. *(ACL Photo)*

Library of Congress Control Number: 2001090217

ISBN 1-883089-62-X

Layout and Design by
Kenneth L. Miller
Miller Design & Photography
Salem, Va. 24153

Printed by
Walsworth Publishing Co.
Marceline, Mo. 64658

TABLE OF CONTENTS

F7 "A" No. 409 and another unidentified F7 "A" bracket an A-B-B-A lashup of FT units on a long freight train a Jacksonville, Florida in the early-1950s.
(ACL Photo)

INTRODUCTION AND ACKNOWLEDGEMENTS

While the author has been a life-long fan of the old Seaboard Air Line Railway, as a rail enthusiast born and raised in Petersburg, Virginia, he also confesses to a more than passing interest in its rival, the Atlantic Coast Line Railroad. After all, it was the good citizens of Petersburg who funded the construction of the ACL's earliest predecessor company—the Petersburg Railroad.

But there was more to admire about the ACL in Petersburg than just its history. For a start, there was its distinctive passenger station that was located downtown on Washington Street, east of my high school and my parent's first home in Petersburg. Then there was "BX" Tower - a frame structure during the steam era and a single story brick building in later years - that controlled the junction on the south side of town between the 6-mile main line cutoff to Ettrick and the tracks leading to downtown. And there was the ACL's Collier Yard, named for the owner of the land on which it was built. Collier was also a former president of the Petersburg Railroad and co-signer of the document that surrendered the City of Petersburg to General U. S. Grant on April 3, 1865. Collier Yard was a small facility during the ACL era that was subsequently expanded by the SCL and then closed by CSXT. Over the years, it has been a popular gathering spot for train watchers as the tracks of the former Norfolk and Western's freight belt line pass under the main line tracks of the former ACL at the north end of the yard. On an afternoon bicycle trip from my home in

In order to route through traffic around Petersburg, Virginia, where the tracks ran for a distance through the downtown streets, the ACL built a 6 mile cutoff in 1895. The cutoff, which became a part of the ACL's main line, was built west of the city and ran from Collier to Dunlop, bridging the main lines of the Seaboard Air Line and Norfolk and Western railroads as well as the Appomattox River. The southern junction of the main line cutoff and the line to downtown Petersburg was located at "BX" Tower, located just north of Collier Yard. Passenger trains ceased to use the downtown line after the new ACL passenger station was opened at Ettrick in 1942, but the line continued in use for many years as an important industrial lead track. H. Reid captured this splendid view as the engine crew on one of the ACL's beautiful Pacifics slowed to pick up orders for their southbound extra at "BX" Tower.
(H. Reid Photo/William E. Griffin, Jr. Collection)

the Walnut Hill section of Petersburg, I was privileged as a youth to view near Collier Yard the train operations of both the N&W's distinctive steam locomotives and the ACL's colorful diesels. What a show!

Join me now as we turn back the clock to take a look at the history of the Atlantic Coast Line Railroad. In telling the story of the ACL, I have been fortunate to have been given access to much of the railroad's archival material. I have also received the kind assistance and support of many contributing friends, photographers and collectors. Without their help this book would not have been possible.

I am especially indebted to David W.

Salter, whose exceptional photographs have appeared in many books and magazines. When I asked for his assistance in finding previously unpublished pictures of the ACL for this book, he graciously came to my aid with extraordinary photos of his own as well as from his extensive collection.

My sincere appreciation is also extended to the following friends and fellow railfans who have made available their photographs and/or photographs from their collection: Russell W. Davis, Henry L. Kitchen, Bruce R. Meyer, David W. Salter, C. K. Marsh, Jr., Harold K. Vollrath, Robert S. Crockett, C. L. Goolsby, Tom G. King, Al M. Langley, Jr., Curt Tillotson, Jr., Jay Williams, Robert H. Hanson, Warren L. Calloway, Carlton N. McKenney, M. Ray Sturges, Evan D. Siler, Mac B. Connery, Frank E. Ardrey, Jr., L. D. Moore, Tal Carey, David George, Mallory Hope Ferrell, Barry Young, Jim Shaw, Ralph Coleman, Charles McIntyre and Gary T. Sease.

From the collections of the abovementioned friends, I am pleased to include photographs in this book that were taken by: H. Reid, Richard O. Sharpless, John B. Allen, George B. Mock, Jr., George W. Pettengill, Jr., R. D. Sharpless, Jr., Walter H. Thrall, James Bowie, J. I. Kelly, Joseph Lavelle, Kenneth M. Ardinger,

Felix Brunot, J. R. Quinn, Oscar W. Kimsey, Jr., C. W. Witbeck, George Votava, Truman Blasingame, Richard Short, Richard Gladulich and William B. Gwaltney.

A special note of thanks also goes to the members of the Old Dominion Chapter of the National Railway Historical Society, who have enthusiastically supported every book that I have ever written.

I would also like to thank the members of the Atlantic Coast Line and Seaboard Air Line Historical Society for their support in this project and for the job that they are doing to preserve the history of these two most interesting railroads. Readers who want to learn more about the ACL, or its affiliated roads, are encouraged to contact the society regarding membership.

William E. Griffin, Jr.
Orange Park, Florida
November 15, 2001

The ACL's downtown passenger station in Petersburg, Virginia (shown here in 1951) was located on Washington Street in the block between Union and Market streets. Just visible in this photo to the left, was the freight station that was located adjacent to the passenger station in the block between Union and Sycamore streets. The tracks began to parallel Washington Street at Perry Street, near the former Brown and Williamson Tobacco Factory, and ran along Washington Street until they turned north at Madison Street to reach the Norfolk and Western passenger station. The Washington Street station ceased to be the principal ACL station at Petersburg when the railroad opened a new North Petersburg station at Ettrick, Virginia in January of 1942. A combination freight and passenger station was built at Ettrick adjacent to the 1942 station in 1956. The ACL Washington Street freight and passenger stations were torn down in 1955 to make way for more shops in downtown Petersburg.

(William E. Griffin, Jr. Collection)

Introduction and acknowledgements

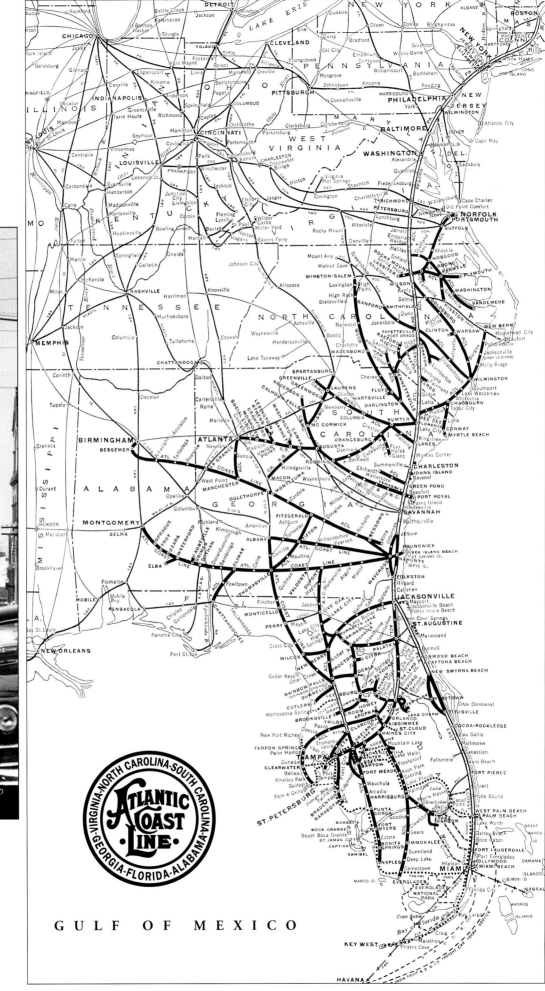

Introduction and acknowledgements   VII

The Atlantic Coast Line Railroad Company (ACL) operated a rail system of over 5,000 miles in the states of Virginia, North Carolina, South Carolina, Georgia, Alabama and Florida. Its principal main line extended between Richmond, Virginia and Jacksonville, Florida, with important secondary main lines diverging there from to reach Norfolk, Virginia and Wilmington, North Carolina, on the east, and Columbia, South Carolina, Augusta and Atlanta, Georgia and Birmingham and Montgomery, Alabama, on the west, with a network of lines extending southwardly from Jacksonville, Florida and from Dupont and Thomasville, Georgia into the Florida peninsula. Approximately 35 percent of the ACL's operated mileage was located in the state of Florida where it primarily served the Central and West Coast areas. Through freight and passenger service were provided to the East Coast of Florida via connections with the Florida East Coast Railway (FEC). The ACL also maintained, through stock ownership or lease, a substantial interest in a number of affiliated rail lines that operated in the South.

The rail system of the ACL was basically formed during the later half of the 19th Century through the merger and acquisition of more than 100 separate railroad companies. During this period, one of the vehicles used to assemble what would eventually become the ACL family of railroads was the Atlantic Coast Line Company, a Connecticut corporation and non-operating holding company that was the railroad's largest single stockholder.

Railroad construction was in its initial stage when the ACL's earliest constituent was formed. That company, the Petersburg Railroad, was incorporated by special act of the General Assembly of Virginia on February 10, 1830, and by special act of the North Carolina legislature on January 1, 1831. The railroad was chartered by the citizens of Petersburg, Virginia for the purpose of "... making a railroad from some point within the corporation of Petersburg, to some convenient point on the North Carolina line... ." It was only the third rail-

road to be chartered in the Commonwealth of Virginia and was the first in the South to be built in a north-south direction.

It was also the South's first interstate railroad and was built by the citizens of Petersburg as another round in the long standing rivalry between the Virginia towns of Petersburg and Norfolk for the commerce of the state of North Carolina. In fact, the location of the ACL Railroad was determined by the physical situation of North Carolina and these two Virginia towns.

In the eighteenth and early nineteenth centuries, the early settlers of southeastern Virginia and northeastern North Carolina built their homes along the navigable waterways that flowed through the tidewater sections of those states. Gradually towns with port facilities were established at the fall line of the rivers where the rocks and swirling rapids marked the upstream limit of navigation. Petersburg and Emporia, Virginia, and Gaston and Raleigh, North Carolina are each located at or near the fall line of a river.

Unlike Virginia, with its series of tributaries and navigable rivers that emptied into the Chesapeake Bay, northeastern North Carolina lacked a deep water port and was plagued by the presence of the Outer Banks and its shifting inlets. As a result, the farmers of northeastern North Carolina were obliged to move their products to the Virginia towns for transport to market. By the late-1820s, construction of the Dismal Swamp Canal had given Norfolk an advantage over Petersburg in the competition for the North Carolina commerce that moved to market via the Roanoke River. Determined to retain the commerce from what they considered to be their rightful trade territory, the citizens of Petersburg decided to build a railroad from their town to a point below the falls of the Roanoke River near Weldon, North Carolina, a distance of 59 miles.

The railroad was built in almost a straight line from Petersburg to Belfield (now Emporia) and sections were put in use as they were completed. The line was originally laid with strap rail and sawmills were erected along the way to provide timbers for bridges and ties for the rails. Much of the

The oldest predecessor of the Atlantic Coast Line Railroad was the Petersburg Railroad Company. On February 10, 1830, the City of Petersburg, Virginia obtained a charter from the General Assembly of the Commonwealth of Virginia to construct a railroad from it name-sake city to some convenient point on the North Carolina line. The railroad was built as a community enterprise to attract trade to the city. The railroad was built in almost a straight line from Petersburg to the Roanoke River and began operations to Belfield (now Emporia) in 1832. The line was opened to Blakely, North Carolina on the north bank of the Roanoke River across from Weldon in 1833, a distance of 59 miles. The railroad did not bridge the Roanoke River to Weldon until 1843. As shown in this early adver-tisement, the Petersburg Railroad participated with the Wilmington and Weldon (another ACL predecessor) and the Raleigh and Gaston railroads for through service between Wilmington, North Carolina and Washington, D. C. North of Petersburg, service to Washington was handled by the Richmond and Petersburg and Richmond, Fredericksburg and Potomac rail-roads. However, this was a through route in name only. There would be no physical connection between these railroads until after the War Between the States. The communities that had expended the funds to build them did not want any traffic to bypass their towns so these early railroads merely operated from terminus to terminus.

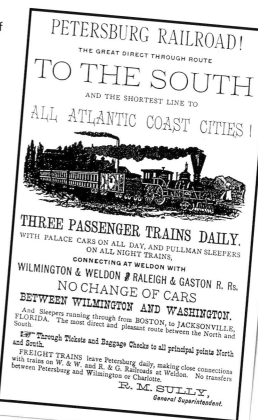

(Russell W. Davis Collection)

grading was performed by slave labor. Operation was opened to Emporia on Christmas Eve, 1832 and the line reached Blakely, North Carolina on the north bank of the Roanoke River, across from Weldon, on October 1, 1833. Freight and passengers were ferried across the river by boat until 1843 when a railroad bridge was finally com-pleted.

Of course, construction of the Petersburg Railroad did not go unnoticed by the citizens of Norfolk. *"We must bestir ourselves, a local newspaper proclaimed, and lay down a railroad of our own to the Roanoke, if we hope to retain a share of this trade."*

On March 8, 1832, the Portsmouth and Roanoke Railroad Company (the earliest pre-decessor line of the Seaboard Air Line Railway) was chartered to build a railroad from Portsmouth and Suffolk, Virginia to the Roanoke River. Thus was born a railroad rivalry that would last for over a hundred years until the merger of the ACL and SAL in 1967.

The Petersburg Railroad was an immediate success and soon other rail lines were char-

tered by citizens who hoped to divert trade to their towns and cities. Just as Petersburg and Norfolk were in competition for the trade of Virginia and northeastern North Carolina, Norfolk and Wilmington, North Carolina likewise competed for the trade of the Carolinas. Charleston, South Carolina was also in competition with Wilmington and Savannah, Georgia for the trade of the upper Pee Dee River sections and the Savannah River valley. The separate railroads that would eventually come together to form the ACL system all had their beginnings as a result of the rivalry for trade advantage between the cities and sections along the South Atlantic Coast.

Another early predecessor company of the Atlantic Coast Line Railroad was chartered in 1836 to build a railroad north of Petersburg to Richmond, Virginia. Construction of this new company—the Richmond and Petersburg Railroad—began in the spring of 1836, and by May 1838 its line was opened from the south bank of the James River at Richmond to Pocahontas, on the north bank of the Appomattox River, across from

Petersburg. Freight and passengers were ferried across the river by boat as the tracks of the two railroads were not joined at Petersburg. In fact, the two railroads initially made no effort to interchange business between their separate lines. They were typical of railroads in the South prior to the War Between the States that built their lines from terminus to terminus with no intention of making a connection with other lines on either end. During this period, railroads were regarded as connections between communities and the investors who had funded their construction had no desire to see their towns converted from terminals to way stations.

To the south, another early ACL predecessor company was being organized in the state of North Carolina. On January 3, 1834 the citizens of Wilmington, North Carolina obtained a charter to build the Wilmington and Raleigh Railroad between its two namesake cities. However, when the citizens of Raleigh failed to subscribe to the capital stock of this road, the proposed route was changed to extend north of Wilmington to Weldon via Goldsboro and Rocky Mount. The 161-mile line was opened to Weldon, near the terminus of the Petersburg Railroad, on March 19, 1840. At the time of completion, it was the longest railroad in the world. In 1855, its name was changed to the Wilmington and Weldon Railroad and at Wilmington the railroad operated its own steamboats to Charleston, South Carolina.

During this time, another early railroad—the Richmond, Fredericksburg and Potomac (RF&P) - was building a rail line north from Richmond to steamboat landings, first at Potomac Creek (1837) and later at Aquia Creek (1842), where connections were made with boats that plied the Potomac River to Washington. In the decade prior to the outbreak of the War Between the States, the RF&P and the three separate railroads that would later become a part of the ACL (which were commonly referred to as the "Weldon Route"), offered the most direct route of travel between the North and Charleston, South Carolina even though none of their lines were physically connected and passengers had to transfer between trains at Richmond, Petersburg and Weldon.

All of these railroads were of strategic importance during the war. After the fall of Norfolk during General George McClellan's Peninsula Campaign and the successful Union blockade of Charleston harbor, Wilmington became the major port serving the northern portion of the Confederacy. During much of the war, Wilmington was the only open port that could be used by blockade runners and the Weldon Route railroads essentially formed the "Bread Line of the Confederacy". However, that strategic location would also make them a target for destruction.

In March of 1864, President Abraham Lincoln appointed Lieutenant General Ulysses S. Grant commander in chief of the armies of the United States with the directive that he finally end the War Between the States by capturing the General Robert E. Lee's Army of Northern Virginia and the capital of the Confederacy at Richmond. Beginning in May of that year, Grant began a relentless campaign to capture Lee's army. Unable to achieve his objective in the battles of the Wilderness, Spotsylvania and Cold Harbor, Grant crossed the James River in June and besieged Lee's army at Petersburg. For the next ten months Grant relentlessly pushed his left flank around Petersburg with the objective of cutting Lee's railroad supply lines from the south. In August of 1864, the Union army captured the Petersburg Railroad's line to Weldon in the vicinity of Globe Tavern, leaving only the Southside Railroad as Petersburg's connection with the rest of the south. That final supply line was broken on April 1, 1865 at the Battle of Five Forks. Evacuating Petersburg and Richmond, Lee retreated westward until overtaken at Appomattox where he surrendered his outnumbered army on April 9, 1865.

At the termination of the War Between the States, the railroads in the South faced appalling conditions. Most of the bridges and track had been torn up and their engines and cars had either been destroyed or worn out. To make matters worse, few of the companies possessed the capital or materials to effect repairs. Their resources largely consisted of bonds and currency of the Confederacy which were entirely worthless. Nevertheless, they set about the task of rebuilding their railroads.

The first order of business for the railroads of the "Weldon Route" was the physical connection of their respective lines. A connection at Richmond between the RF&P and the Richmond and Petersburg was achieved in May of 1867. In August of that same year, the Richmond and Petersburg bridged the Appomattox River to connect with the Petersburg Railroad. At that time, the Petersburg Railroad was physically connected to the Wilmington and Weldon Railroad via trackage rights over the Seaboard and Roanoke Railroad's bridge over the Roanoke River. With their lines now physically joined, the separate rail companies were able to offer through joint routes for passenger and freight trains between New York and the South. This led to an immediate increase in traffic and prompted Northerners to boost their investment in the southern railroads. It was during this period that Northern capitalists gained control of these roads from the communities that had originally financed their construction. This period also marked the beginning of the formation of the Atlantic Coast Line system.

In December of 1867, a group of prominent investors from Baltimore, Maryland, headed by William T. Walters and B. F. Newcomer, began to purchase shares of stock in the Wilmington and Weldon. Within a year, they owned enough stock to have a controlling interest in the railroad. Walters group then set their sights on another Wilmington railroad - the Wilmington and Manchester. This 163-mile line had been chartered in 1853 to attract trade from the interior of South Carolina to the port of Wilmington. Its line extended from a point on the Cape Fear River opposite Wilmington via Florence to a connection with the South Carolina Railroad near Kingville, South Carolina. Built to a five-foot gauge to correspond with the track of the South Carolina Railroad, it was in a deplorable state by the end of the War Between the States and declared bankruptcy in 1868. Walters group acquired the Wilmington and Manchester and it was reorganized in 1870 as the Wilmington, Columbia and Augusta Railroad.

But William Walters' objective was much greater than the acquisition of the railroads at Wilmington, North Carolina. A native of Pennsylvania, Walters moved to Baltimore in 1841 and made his fortune as a produce commission merchant. A Confederate sympathizer, he and his family lived in Europe during the War Between the States. He returned to Baltimore after the war and resumed the direct management of his produce commission business. As a commission merchant, Walters was very knowledgeable of the issues surrounding the shipment of produce to the eastern markets. In the years prior to the War Between the States, fruits and vegetables were grown on the farms of eastern North Carolina and Tidewater Virginia and shipped via steamboats that plied the Chesapeake Bay to Baltimore or the Atlantic Ocean to New York. Walters knew that the climate around the Wilmington area was conducive to the growth of fruits and vegetables to maturity a full three to four weeks earlier than the existing producers. All that was needed for this expansion of the produce market was a fast and dependable mode of transportation. Walters saw the railroads as a means to develop this commerce.

Using the Wilmington and Weldon as its hub, the Walters group began to acquire connecting roads to the north and south such as the Northeastern Railroad of South Carolina (between Charleston and Florence), the Wilmington, Columbia and Augusta (Wilmington to Columbia) and the Cheraw and Darlington (Florence to Cheraw). In 1871, they joined with an affiliate of the Pennsylvania Railroad to also acquire control of the Richmond and Petersburg.

By the end of the decade the Petersburg Railroad would also be brought into the system. After the separate rail lines had been physically joined, the Petersburg Railroad became a middle link in the system. It originated and terminated little traffic and was vulnerable to competition at Weldon from the SAL predecessor, the Seaboard and Roanoke. The Petersburg had been using the Seaboard and Roanoke's bridge over the Roanoke River and its tracks between Garysburg and Weldon since the end of the war and, to strengthen its position, the Petersburg built its own bridge over the river in 1872. However, hampered by continued local control and declining revenues, the Petersburg faced one financial crisis after another until it was placed in receivership in 1877. The railroad was then put under common management with the Richmond and Petersburg and the two companies entered into an agreement that coordinated their operations with the Walters system of railroads.

William Walters and his associates now had control of a route of affiliated rail lines between Richmond, Virginia and Charleston, South Carolina and, by means of their friendly connections with the RF&P and Pennsylvania railroads, could offer through service between the Northeast and Charleston. It was during this period that the railroads which made up the "Weldon Route" began to be referred to as the "Atlantic Coast Line". The name was selected because their through routes closely paralleled the Atlantic Ocean. However, it was only a trademark name at that time and was used merely to designate a route. Each railroad retained its own name and separate corporate identity, but was operated under a unified plan of overall management.

The task of centralizing the managements became the job of 36-year old Henry Walters, the only son of William T. Walters. Educated at Georgetown University and the Lawrence Scientific School at Harvard University, he gained his railroad experience in the engineering corps of the Valley Railroad of Virginia and in the operating department of the Pittsburgh & Connellsville Railroad. In 1884, the Atlantic Coast Line Association was formed with William Walters as chairman of the Board of Directors and Executive Committee and Henry Walters as General Manager of the Executive Department.

The Walters group expended substantial funds to upgrade the railroads and in 1885 construction began on what came to be known as the "Fayetteville cut-off". Prior to the construction of this trackage, the main line of the Atlantic Coast Line extended from Rocky Mount, North Carolina on the Wilmington and Weldon Railroad to Florence, South Carolina on the Wilmington, Columbia and Augusta Railroad via Wilmington, North Carolina. Between 1885 and 1893, a new line was built from Contentnea, near Wilson, North Carolina, via Fayetteville, to Pee Dee, near Florence, South Carolina. When finally opened for service on January 1, 1893, the "cut-off" line materially reduced the running time of trains between Richmond and Florence as it was 62 miles shorter than the line through Wilmington. Soon the route via the "Fayetteville Cut-off" became a part of the principal main line of the railroad.

Another important step was taken in 1886 to speed the flow of through traffic when the tracks of the "Atlantic Coast Line" railroads in the Carolinas were all converted to standard gauge. Prior to 1886, the railroads north of Wilmington were operating on tracks that were built on what had come to be termed the standard gauge of 4 feet 8 1/2 inches. However, the railroads south of Wilmington were operating on tracks that had been built to a gauge of 5 feet. As a

result, it was necessary to change the trucks under all freight cars that were moving through Wilmington. On a single day in 1886, all of the trackage south of Wilmington was converted to standard gauge. Similarly, much of the five-foot equipment was rewheeled to standard gauge that same day.

These improvements enabled Walters to achieve his avowed objective to create an all-rail line to New York and intermediate markets for the transportation of fresh produce. In 1888, a through fast freight service known as the *Atlantic Coast Despatch* was inaugurated for the movement of fruit and vegetables in train loads from the South to the northern markets. The service was an immediate success and marked the beginning of this traffic as an important tonnage for the railroads.

A significant advance in passenger train service was also established during 1888. In January of that year, the *New York and Florida Special,* an electric-lighted, steam-heated all-Pullman vestibule train commenced operation three times a week between New York and Jacksonville, Florida on a schedule of 30 hours and 15 minutes. As was the case with the *Atlantic Coast Despatch*, this train operated over the Pennsylvania Railroad, Washington Southern, RF&P and the "Atlantic Coast Line" railroads between New York and Charleston, South Carolina. Between Charleston and Jacksonville, the train operated over the lines of the Plant System railroads.

The through operations of perishable freight trains and passengers trains would soon result in the transformation of a small group of independently operated railroads into one of the great railroad systems of the country. Realizing that cooperation among the separate railroads was essential in order to provide the dependable service required for through traffic, the Walters group formed a holding company known as the American Improvement and Construction Company in 1889. This syndicate, which would become the Atlantic Coast Line Company in 1893, began to exercise control over the management of the separate railroad companies.

During this period, the Atlantic Coast Line also opened an important new line to the port of Norfolk, Virginia. Initiated by two predecessor companies, the Western Branch Railway and the Chowan & Southern Railroad Company, the Norfolk and Carolina

In 1869, a group of Baltimore, Maryland capitalists headed by William T. Walters acquired a controlling interest in the Wilmington and Weldon Railroad. Using the Wilmington and Weldon as a holding company, the Walters group then gained control of its connecting roads to the north and south. Initially, these affiliated roads were referred to as "The Weldon Route", but by 1871 they were called the "Atlantic Coast Line" because their route so closely paralleled the Atlantic Coast. When William Walters died in 1894, his son Henry—shown here in a company portrait—was chosen president of the associated railroads and took control of their affairs. From their offices in New York City, Walters and his associate, Benjamin Newcomer, directed the operation of the railroads and in 1900 merged them into one corporation, the Atlantic Coast Line Railroad. Henry Walters was elected Chairman of the Board of Directors of the ACL and served in that capacity until his death in 1931.

(ACL Photo)

Railroad Company completed a 100-mile line from Pinners Point, Virginia to Tarboro, North Carolina on April 1, 1890. At that time, the Norfolk and Carolina was operated as a subsidiary of the Atlantic Coast Line, connecting with the Wilmington and Weldon s line from Rocky Mount at Tarboro. While it did not significantly alter the routing of freight traffic over the system, it did provide an important new line for the movement of perishables via the *Atlantic Coast Despatch* from the South through Pinners Point to the Pennsylvania Railroad's new terminal at Port Norfolk.

In 1893, William Walters stepped down as the president of the Atlantic Coast Line Association (he passed away the following year) and the position passed to Henry Walters, who would remain the central figure in the railroad's affairs until his death in 1931. At the same time that Henry Walters was assuming full control over the affairs of the Coast Line properties, another major rail system was forming in the Southeast. In 1894, the vast network of railroads that had been organized by Thomas Clyde and his son, William, under the holding company known as the Richmond and West Point Terminal Railway and Warehouse Company, was reorganized and consolidated in 1894 by the Drexel, Morgan and Company as the Southern Railway Company.

Henry Walters wisely established a friendly relationship with J. Pierpont Morgan, the New York banker whose firm controlled the Southern, and with Samuel Spencer, the Southern's first president. These relationships proved to be beneficial to both companies, especially in their competition with the third major rail system, the Seaboard Air Line, that was then emerging in the Southeast. In a co-operative transaction that was particularly egregious to the Seaboard, in 1896 the Coast Line gave the Southern Railway access to Port Norfolk by granting it trackage rights over the Wilmington and Weldon from Selma to Tarboro, North Carolina and over the Norfolk and Carolina from Tarboro to Pinners Point, Virginia. The Seaboard responded by extending its main line from Norlina, North Carolina to Richmond, Virginia, thus solidifying its position as a major competitor to both the ACL and Southern railway systems.

As the turn of the century approached, it was clear that the era of the small independent railroad companies had come to an end in the South. Three major systems were being formed that would dominate the railroad landscape in the future. The time has come for Henry Walters to begin the process of consolidating the rail lines that would form the Atlantic Coast Line Railroad.

In 1898, the General Assembly of the Commonwealth of Virginia approved the purchase of the Petersburg Railroad by the Richmond and Petersburg Railroad. The 82-mile railroad created by this transaction was named the "Atlantic Coast Line Railroad Company of Virginia". That same year, the state legislature of the South Carolina granted a charter to a new company named the "Atlantic Coast Line Railroad Company of South Carolina", to consolidate the rail lines of the Wilmington, Columbia and Augusta, the Northeastern Railroad Company of South Carolina, the Cheraw and Darlington, the Manchester and Augusta, and the Florence Railroad.

The following year, the Atlantic Coast Line Railroad Company of South Carolina

From the earliest days of its corporate history in the 1880s, the ACL had located its headquarters at Wilmington, North Carolina. Prior to 1885, the principal route of the Atlantic Coast Line had been from Richmond, Virginia to Wilmington, thence to Florence and Charleston, South Carolina. In 1885, the Wilmington and Weldon Railroad constructed the Fayetteville cut-off from Contentnea, North Carolina to Fayetteville, and thence, later, to Pee Dee, South Carolina on the Wilmington, Columbia and Augusta Railroad. This new line significantly shortened the running time between Richmond and Jacksonville and became the ACL's main line. Even though Wilmington was removed from the main line by the "Fayetteville cut-off", the railroad's general offices remained in that city until the summer of 1960. The general office complex consisted of four separate buildings designated as "A", "B", "C" and "D". The Accounting Department occupied buildings "A" and "B", while the distinctive building "C"—shown here in a 1928 photograph—housed the principal general offices and the waiting room for the passenger station. The remaining corporate functions were accommodated in building "D". The intersection of Red Cross and Front Streets in downtown Wilmington was almost surrounded by the ACL buildings, each connected to the other by overstreet walkways.

(ACL Photo)

entered into a transaction that would be valuable to the ACL for many years. On August 9, 1899, it entered into a joint lease of the properties of the Georgia Railroad with the Louisville and Nashville Railroad. In conjunction with its control of the Charleston and Western Carolina Railroad, the lease of the Georgia Railroad gave the ACL an important entry into Atlanta, Georgia. The C&WC had been formed in 1896 and quickly came under ACL control in 1897. The ACL's Manchester & Augusta Railroad line from Sumter, South Carolina connected with the C&WC at Robbins, South Carolina. The C&WC granted trackage rights to the ACL over the 29 miles of its line from Robbins to

Augusta. At Augusta, connection was made with the Georgia Railroad for the routing of traffic to Atlanta.

Effective May 1, 1900, the Atlantic Coast Line Railroad Company of South Carolina, the Wilmington and Weldon Railroad, the Norfolk and Carolina Railroad, and the 11-mile South Eastern Railroad, were merged into the *Atlantic Coast Line Railroad Company of Virginia*. On that date, the name of the company was changed by action of its stockholders to the Atlantic Coast Line Railroad Company. This new railroad had over 1600 miles of main line tracks extending from Richmond and Norfolk, Virginia to Charleston, South Carolina, with various branch and feeder lines in Virginia and the Carolinas.

However, at the same time that Henry Walters was consolidating all of the separately organized connecting lines south of Richmond, he was required to relinquish the ACL's control of the RF&P Railroad. The RF&P was the ACL's connecting line at Richmond. It owned a rail line from Richmond to Quantico, Virginia, where connection was made with the Washington Southern Railway, a railroad controlled by the Pennsylvania Railroad.

In April of 1900, the new Seaboard Air Line Railway was created by the consolidation of a group of associated railroads that had been operating over 900 miles of trackage in the Carolinas and Georgia. Shortly thereafter the line was completed to Richmond. However, when this new railroad, that had been created by John Skelton Williams and his banking associates, was denied desirable traffic arrangements by the ACL-controlled RF&P, it petitioned the Virginia General Assembly for the authority to build a new railroad parallel to the RF&P between Richmond and the Potomac River. To the chagrin of the ACL and RF&P, the General Assembly not only granted Williams the charter for a new railroad, it also passed an act authorizing the sale of the Commonwealth's holdings of the RF&P's Common Stock and Dividend Obligations. The ACL and RF&P quickly acquiesced and came to terms with Williams. The SAL abandoned its proposal to build a new railroad with the understanding that the facilities of the RF&P would be enlarged and the SAL's traffic would be handled by the RF&P on the same terms and conditions that applied to the traffic of the ACL.

The SAL constructed a connection with the RF&P at a point called Hermitage and interchange of traffic between the two companies commenced on July 1, 1900. To carry out the plan that had been reached as a result of the negotiations with the SAL, on July 31, 1901, the Pennsylvania Railroad, Atlantic Coast Line Railroad, Southern Railway, Chesapeake and Ohio Railway, Seaboard Air Line Railway and the Baltimore and Ohio Railway entered into an agreement to form the Richmond-Washington Company, a New Jersey Corporation, in which each railroad would have an equal interest. The Richmond-Washington Company acquired all of the stock of the Washington Southern

Railway and a majority of the voting stock of the RF&P. Thereafter, the RF&P and the Washington Southern would be operated as the "Richmond-Washington Line", under one management. The traffic of all six of the railroad partners would be handled over the RF&P and Washington Southern with "equal promptness and upon equal terms". The ACL was required to relinquish its control over the RF&P and the Pennsylvania similarly relinquished its control over the Washington Southern. On November 1, 1901, the management of the Washington Southern was turned over to the officers of the RF&P, and the two railroads were operated as a unit with separate accounting and records until 1920 when the WS was merged into the RF&P. With the RF&P question resolved in 1901, the ACL turned its attention to its southern connection.

The ACL's connection at Charleston was the Savannah, Florida and Western Railway Company, the flagship company of Henry B. Plant's system of railroads. A native of Connecticut, Plant had been a successful superintendent of the Adams Express Company prior to the War Between the States. Soon after the war commenced, Plant assumed control of the former Adams Express Company business in the Confederate states and established the Southern Express Company. However, unlike the Walters family, Plant was not sympathetic to the Confederacy and remained in the South merely to conduct the business affairs of the express company. He also spent time in Europe during the war and returned to the South at the end of the hostilities to resume the business of the Southern Express Company. He also entered the railroad business in 1879 when he acquired the Atlantic and Gulf Railroad, that was then operating between Savannah and Bainbridge, Georgia. Plant reorganized this company to form the Savannah, Florida and Western Railway.

Over the next twenty years, Plant acquired a number of railroads in the states of Florida, Georgia and Alabama, eventually forming a 1600-mile system with main lines from Charleston, South Carolina to Port Tampa, Florida and from Savannah, Georgia to Montgomery, Alabama, and numerous branch and feeder lines in the states of South Carolina, Georgia, Florida and Alabama. Along with the Savannah, Florida and Western, other major components of the Plant System included the South Florida

After the railroads were returned to their owners by the United States Railroad Administration following the First World War, the ACL began an extensive program to improve the physical plant of its railroad. Millions of dollars were spent for double track, heavy rail, ballast, new motive power and equipment. In the fall of 1925 double track was completed on the main line between Richmond and Jacksonville, with automatic signals installed concurrent with the track construction. The grading work for the double tracking was performed by laborers using dirt moving scoops drawn by mule teams. This 1920s photo shows laborer wheelers grading the line for new ACL double track at White Hall, South Carolina just north of Yemassee.

(ACL Photo)

(Sanford to Port Tampa), the Jacksonville, Tampa and Key West (Jacksonville to Sanford), Charleston and Savannah, Brunswick and Western (Brunswick via Waycross to Albany, Georgia) and the Alabama Midland (Bainbridge to Montgomery, Alabama). Plant also organized a steamship line that operated from Port Tampa to Key West, Havana, Mobile and the West Indies and hotels that were the finest resorts on the west coast of Florida. Plant developed and promoted the west coast and central section of Florida in the same manner that Henry Flagler had improved the east coast of the Sunshine State.

Plant passed away in the summer of 1899, just a few months prior to his 80th birthday. During the later years of his life, he had created an vast business empire which included an extensive railroad network in the South, especially in the state of Florida. Plant had desired that his system of railroads remain independent and so specified in a codicil to

his will. However, his heirs desired to liquidate their holdings in the separate companies as quickly as possible and petitioned a court to set aside the trust provisions of his will. Those trust provisions were set aside by the Supreme Court of New York in January of 1902 and Henry Walters immediately began discussions with the Plant family about the possibly of the sale of the Plant System of railroads to the ACL. After complex negotiations, the ACL was able to acquire the Plant System and its leased lines and subsidiaries, plus steamship lines and hotels in April of 1902. The acquisition of the Plant System of railroads added over 1600 miles of trackage to the ACL and established the Coast Line's basic system that would exist for the next forty-five years.

However, while the ACL would not make a substantial increase to the mileage of its basic system until 1946, it continued to extend its reach after the turn of the century by the acquisition of control or lease of a

The grading has been completed and ties have been laid for the new second track at White Hall, South Carolina. Now the maintenance crews await the arrival of the rail laying forces and exchange a greeting with the engine crew of a northbound extra perishable train that storms past behind a Class P-5-B Pacific.

(ACL Photo)

number of affiliated railroads. The most important of the separately-operated properties that affiliated with the ACL was the Louisville and Nashville Railroad. In 1902, the ACL gained control of the L&N when it acquired 51% of its stock. Control of the L&N also gave the ACL control of the L&N's subsidiary, the Nashville, Chattanooga and St. Louis Railway. The ACL already held a joint lease, along with the L&N, of the Georgia Railroad & Banking Company (and its affiliated lines the Atlanta and West Point, and the Western Railway of Alabama). In 1923, the ACL and L&N also jointly leased the 309-mile Carolina, Clinchfield & Ohio Railroad for a term of 999 years. Three other railroads controlled by the ACL through stock ownership included the 75-mile Columbia, Newberry & Laurens Railroad, the 343-mile Charleston & Western Carolina Railway and, the 640-mile Atlanta, Birmingham and Atlantic (later known as the AB&C). Taken together, the ACL and its affiliated family group of railroads comprised a system of over 12,000

operated miles, making it one of the largest in the Unites States.

With its basic system in place, the ACL turned its attention to upgrading and improving the physical condition of its entire transportation plant. Initially, the railroad focused on its main line between Richmond and Jacksonville. Construction of a second main line began in 1904 and was continued each year. Double track was first installed at locations where it could relieve congestion caused by heavy traffic at important junctions and terminals. The progress of double tracking and many other improvement projects were slowed during the years of World War I, during which time the ACL and other American railroads were placed under control of the federal government. However, with the end of the war and release of the railroads from government control in 1920, the projects were intensified such that the double track of the line between Richmond and Jacksonville was completed in the Fall of 1925. Two high-den-

After the turn of the century, the ACL grew rapidly into a large system of leased and/or wholly owned railroads. When it acquired the Plant System of railroads in 1902, it was able to expand from Charleston, South Carolina into the states of Georgia and Florida. After the Plant System was acquired, the ACL progressed Henry Walters goal to establish a direct route from South Florida via the west coast of the state to Georgia, thence to the Midwest and West. In 1925, the ACL began construction of a 40-mile cut-off line between Perry and Monticello, Florida. In this photo, an Erie steam shovel is at work loading dirt onto rail cars on April 13, 1926 during the construction of the Perry-Monticello cut-off. When completed in December of 1926, the cut-off connected the gap in the ACL's line between Thomasville, Georgia and Dunellon, Florida, thereby significantly shortening the ACL's route from Florida to the Midwest.

(ACL Photo)

sity segments of track between Jacksonville and Tampa were also double tracked at this time. One such section was located south of Jacksonville between Moncrief and Yukon and the other was an 11-mile section between Orange City Junction and Sanford.

Millions of dollars were spent by the ACL on the Richmond and Jacksonville double track project, which also included the laying of heavier 100-lb. rail and stone ballast, improving drainage and track alignments, and the strengthening of bridges. Automatic block signals were also installed concurrent with the improvements to the track structure. These improvements were made during the height of the Florida boom period of the mid-1920s and enabled the railroad to enjoy increased revenues year after year. It was a time when the ACL established many new passenger trains to attract passengers to Florida from both the Northeast and the Midwest. As a result, the ACL was also

required to step up its expenditures for new motive power, rolling stock, stations and shop facilities. Yards were enlarged at many key locations and, due to the large concentration of motive power and rolling stock in Florida, major new shops were built at Uceta, near Tampa. These new shops joined the existing shops at Rocky Mount and Waycross as the major repair facilities on the railroad.

The ACL also built a number of new lines on the central and western coast of Florida during the 1920s to tap new business and smooth the flow of traffic to and from that region. The most important of these was the 40-mile Perry to Monticello, Florida Cut-Off that was completed in 1927. Construction of this line connected the existing lines from Thomasville, Georgia to Monticello and from Dunellon, Florida to Perry. The project also included the construction of a 60-mile stretch of double track from Dunellon

As the ACL grew, several large shops were built around its system to provide for the repair and maintenance of the railroad's large fleet of motive power and rolling stock. The largest and most important shops were located at South Rocky Mount, North Carolina. Opened in 1893, these shops were eventually named the Emerson Shops in honor of Thomas M. Emerson, who served as president of the ACL from 1906 to 1913. By the early 1900s, they had become the major shop facility on the system. At the height of its operations the Emerson Shops employed about 2,000 people who repaired, maintained, built and rebuilt both the ACL's locomotives and the rolling stock. In this photo, we see the new north wing of the passenger car shop. At this shop, passenger cars could be built from the ground up and specialty shops performed painting, upholstery and cabinetry.

(ACL Photo)

south to Vitis. Upon its completion, northbound traffic from Tampa no longer had to be routed via Lakeland to Jacksonville. The Perry Cut-Off gave the ACL a new short line route for traffic from the West Coast of Florida via Thomasville, Georgia to the West and Midwest. The other lines built during this period included routes from Haines City to Moore Haven via Sebring, thence to Immokalee and Everglades; Fort Meyers to Collier City; and, Bradenton to Sarasota.

However, even as those lines were being built, the Florida boom was beginning to fizzle. Speculative development outpaced available buyers and suddenly property values were in decline. Then, in September of 1926, a devastating hurricane came ashore in the vicinity of Miami, wrecking havoc on that area and causing Lake Okeechobee to overflow its western banks, ravaging the town of

Moore Haven and killing hundreds of its residents.

The Florida boom had burst, and on its heals would follow the Great Depression of the 1930s. For the next decade, the ACL would face its greatest challenges since the era of Reconstruction. And it would have to confront those tribulations without Henry Walters. The man who had created the ACL System and led it into the new century passed away at the age of 83 in 1931. His nephew, Lyman Delano, was elected to succeed him as the chairman of the board, signaling that the Walters family was still firmly in control of the railroad. Delano was no stranger to ACL operations. In fact, he had been involved in the management of the railroad since 1910 and, as its executive vice president, had been running the railroad for Henry Walters for a number of years. As chairman of the board for both the ACL and the L&N, he continued Walters' practice of requiring that all policy matters affecting the railroads be decided by the chairman.

However, Delano faced a daunting task. By 1930, many of the American railroads, including the ACL's southern connection—the FEC—were bankrupt and in the hands of receivers. Further, with more than one-third of its railroad located in the state of Florida, the ACL was particularly impacted when the national business depression came so closely after the collapse of the Florida boom period. By 1932, tourism had sharply declined and freight revenues plummeted to a third of those earned in the mid-1920s. Delano had to maintain an adequate financial position in spite of the low level of traffic. He suspended dividends on common stock, slashed capital spending, reduced wages and made massive reductions in the work force. During the worst of the Depression—the years 1932-1933—the ACL also discontinued the operation of a large number of local or short-haul passenger trains. They were harsh measures to be sure, but the ACL was able to weather the Great Depression without falling into bankruptcy.

Business conditions began to improve by 1937 and two years later the ACL resumed the purchase of new equipment and the maintenance of its roadway and track structure that had been deferred during the worst of the Depression years. Spurred on by competition from the SAL, the ACL also began to air-condition its passenger equipment and acquired new diesel power and streamlined lightweight cars for its new train, *The Champion*. The name of this new train, selected from over 100,000 entries submitted during a national contest, was also the name of the ACL's vice president of passenger service, Champion McDowell ("Champ") Davis. The train was not named for Davis, but it may not have been a coincidence that the name "Champion" was selected. Certainly, he was the railroad's rising star at that time.

Born in Hickory, North Carolina, Davis entered the service of the ACL predecessor Wilmington and Weldon Railroad in 1893 as a messenger when he was 15 years old. He worked his way up through the Traffic Department as a clerk, stenographer, freight-rate clerk, chief clerk and assistant general freight agent. By 1916 he had become the General Freight Agent for the entire ACL sys-

tem. He was then successively promoted to Freight Traffic Manager, Traffic Vice President, Vice President and Executive Vice President. On October 15, 1942, at age 61, he became the President of the ACL. A bachelor, Davis devoted his entire life to the Episcopal Church and the ACL Railroad.

During his tenure, the ACL was transformed into one of the most modern railroads in the country. A comprehensive program of rehabilitation and modernization of the physical property was begun in 1943, which included the adoption of 131-lb. rail (later 132-lb. rail) as the standard for principal main lines. For important secondary main lines, a standard of 115-lb. section rail was adopted. At the same time as the adoption of the heavier rail as standard, a program of reballasting, retimbering, resurfacing, as well as extensive bridge and trestle work was scheduled over the system progressively. By the end of 1952, the entire double-track main line between Richmond and Jacksonville had been completely relaid with new 131-132 lb. rail, resurfaced on crushed granite ballast and for the most part retimbered with larger creosoted cross-ties.

A second, but almost distinctly different rehabilitation and modernization program was initiated with the acquisition of the Atlanta, Birmingham and Coast Railroad on January 1, 1946. The physical plant of the AB&C was in poor condition when acquired by the ACL, but its lines reached the important gateway cities of Atlanta and Birmingham and could serve as a bridge line between those points and Florida as well as other portions of the Southeast served by the ACL. Hence, the ACL designated the AB&C as its new Western District and instituted an extensive program to bring the railroad up to the ACL's standard for secondary main lines.

The ACL also modernized its signal system. The existing automatic block system with semaphore-type signals was replaced with new coded track circuits and automatic block signaling, with approach-lighting searchlight-type signals, respaced for train speeds up to 100 miles per hour, and with Centralized Traffic Control through certain high traffic density segments. The modern signals were also extended to the former AB&C lines that had not been equipped with signals prior its acquisition by the ACL.

The ACL dramatically modernized its fleet of motive power and rolling stock between the 1939 and 1953 even though the equipment program had to be suspended during the war years. With the end of the conflict, the ACL swiftly dieselized its motive power fleet acquiring 564 new diesel-electrics at a cost in excess of $81 million by the end of 1952. During that same period, the ACL also spent $59 million to acquire more than 19,500 new freight cars. Another $14 million was spent on 146 new passenger train cars, that included lightweight coaches, sleeping cars, dining, lounge and various combination cars.

By 1953, the ACL had made astonishing progress. It had completely dieselized its motive power fleet; owned the largest fleet of rolling bearing equipped freight cars of any railroad in the country; owned one of the most modern fleets of passenger train equipment of the important passenger-carrying roads; had extended the lengths of important passing sidings; improved and expanded important yards; abandoned more than 430 miles of unprofitable branch lines; and, possessed roadway, signal and track structures that enabled high-speed freight and passenger operations on its principal and important secondary main lines. Since the 1930s, the ACL had been boasting in its advertisements that it was the "standard rail-

road of the South". By the mid-1950s, it could certainly back up that claim.

When he retired in July of 1957 at the age of 78, Champ Davis turned over to his successor a railroad that was in superior physical condition. He had been relentless throughout his presidency in his efforts to rehabilitate and modernize the railroad. Perhaps his greatest disappointment was the ACL's unsuccessful bid to acquire the Florida East Coast Railway—a struggle that was waged for 13 years at the Interstate Commerce Commission and in the federal court system. However, the setback in that area paled in comparison to his achievement of transforming the ACL in such a short period into one of the most modern railroad systems in the country.

When he retired, "Champ" Davis had been an employee of the ACL and its predecessor companies for 64 1/2 years. His successor had never worked a day as an ACL employee. However, he was no stranger to the ACL. The man selected by the ACL's Board of Directors to replace Davis was W. Thomas Rice, the 45 year old president of the RF&P Railroad.

Tom Rice was a native of Westmoreland County, Virginia and had graduated from Virginia Polytechnic Institute with a degree in civil engineering. After graduation, he

Freight cars were also built, repaired and maintained by the Car Department at the Emerson Shops. Here we see carmen of the Rip Track Unit at work stenciling a freshly painted ACL boxcar. Freight cars that were repaired at South Rocky Mount had "SRM" stenciled on their sides.
(ACL Photo)

ATLANTIC
COAST
DESPATCH

Top: In the Erecting Shop at South Rocky Mount, workmen could completely dismantle, repair and rebuild steam locomotives for the Northern Division. A separate Back Shop was reserved for major repairs and there was also a shop for work on pistons, valves and crossheads. This is a 1928 interior view of the Boiler Shop, showing locomotives in various stages of boiler maintenance.

Above: Eventually, the ACL concentrated all of its major passenger car work at the Emerson Shops in South Rocky Mount and all of its major freight car work at Waycross, Georgia. Carmen are rebuilding wooden freight cars at Waycross in the circa-1920s photograph.

Left: To repair and maintain the large fleet of motive power and rolling stock concentrated in Florida, the ACL built a major new shop at Uceta, near Tampa, Florida in 1926. These shops had the capability to perform major repairs on locomotives and in this view we are looking in a southeast direction at the new Tampa shops.

(All: ACL Photo)

In 1938, the ACL purchased twelve 4-8-4 steam locomotives from Baldwin Locomotive Works to power the railroad's Florida tourist trains on its main line between Richmond, Virginia and Jacksonville, Florida. These powerful locomotives could handle 20 car trains on fast passenger schedules and were equipped with large tenders which enabled the trains to run straight through without change of motive power. Advertised as the largest engines in the South, they kept the ACL's passenger trains competitive and delayed, albeit briefly, the advent of the diesel era on the Coast Line. Class R-1 4-8-4 No. 1804 rides the turntable at the RF&P's Acca Engine Terminal in Richmond, Virginia.

(Henry L. Kitchen Photo)

A Brief History

Starting his railroad career as a messenger boy with the Wilmington and Weldon Railroad on March 1, 1889, Champion McDowell Davis rose progressively through the ranks of various departments to become the ACL's president on October 15, 1942. When he retired on July 1, 1957 at the age of 79, he had spent more than 64 years of his life in the service of the ACL and its predecessor, the Wilmington and Weldon. Under his tenure, the ACL was transformed into one of the most modern railroads in the Unites States.

(ACL Photo/William E. Griffin Jr. Collection)

was employed by the Pennsylvania Railroad and held several positions in its Operating Department. With the outbreak of the Second World War, he was called to active duty as an officer in the Railway Operating Battalion and was promoted to Lieutenant Colonel in command of the Iranian State Railway. He later served in the European and Pacific Theaters, where he was awarded the Legion of Merit with Oak Leaf Cluster. By the time he was elected president of the ACL, he had risen to the rank of Brigadier General of the Reserve Corps of the United States Army and was the Deputy Commander of the Military Railway Service Headquarters. He would eventually rise to the rank of Major General and serve as Director General of the Transportation Railway Service.

When Tom Rice returned to the United

States followed World War II, he was employed by the RF&P Railroad, where he was appointed the Superintendent of Potomac Yard. He then served as the RF&P's General Superintendent and, beginning in 1955, as its President. His experience with the RF&P gave him with a unique opportunity to learn about the operations of the ACL and the other roads that handled traffic over the RF&P and through its gateway at Potomac Yard.

While he would maintain his predecessor's pursuit for excellence in the ACL's operations and maintenance of its physical plant, Tom Rice brought a new style to the railroad. Whereas Davis had tended to be autocratic, Rice favored a more participatory approach to management. Daily conferences were conducted with managers to review the current status of the railroad. Managers were encouraged to share their ideas and recommendations for improvements. They were also held accountable for their performance. Rice also attempted to improve community relations and promoted the railroad as a cooperative neighbor at town hall meetings held throughout the area of its operation. He also staffed a public relations department that launched a campaign to promote the ACL's efficient passenger and freight service. "Thanks For Using Coast Line" was adopted as a company slogan and was soon painted on the sides of the railroad's rolling stock. Building upon the achievements of Davis, Rice continued to run a well-organized railroad but one that was also more open to its employees and the public.

One Davis initiative that Rice saw to a conclusion was the relocation of the railroad's corporate offices from Wilmington. The board of directors had approved the funding for new corporate offices in Jacksonville in 1957 and groundbreaking ceremonies for the new 17-story building were held in 1958. Construction was completed early in 1960 and the railroad's various departments were sequentially relocated to the new building between July and August of that year.

Shortly after Rice assumed the presidency

As steam locomotives were replaced by diesels, the ACL established a system of shops for diesel general repair, heavy maintenance and inspection. By the early 1950s, the heavy maintenance and general repair on diesels was performed by the shops at Rocky Mount, Waycross and Tampa. Diesel inspection and maintenance work was performed at the shops located at Rocky Mount, North Carolina; Florence, South Carolina; Manchester and Waycross, Georgia; Jacksonville, Lakeland and Tampa, Florida. E6-A No. 519, stenciled for service on the *Florida Special* is shown in the first stage of overhaul at the Jacksonville shops in 1943. The locomotive is on a Whiting Hoist that was used to remove all four of the traction motors in one operation.

(ACL Photo)

18

On January 9, 1888, the *New York and Florida Special* commenced operation between New York and Jacksonville three days a week on a schedule of 30 hours and 15 minutes. Its inauguration was planned to coincide with the opening in St. Augustine of the Ponce DeLeon Hotel, the first of the great Florida resort establishments. The first electrically lighted, vestibuled and steamheated train ever operated in the United States, it consisted of four Pullman sleeping cars, a dining car and a baggage car which housed the dynamo for the electric lights. By 1895 it was operating daily except Sunday and still later on a daily basis, the train continued for eighty-four years each winter season as the ultimate in luxurious train travel between New York and Florida. *The Florida Special* made its first run to Miami on January 9, 1909 and, on January 9, 1941, the City celebrated that event. A huge 7-foot birthday cake was presented to the ACL's general passenger traffic manager by "Miss Florida Special" Frankie Farrington, (shown in this photo with the cake and train) and members of the Miami Chamber of Commerce. This was just one of many such celebrations that were conducted over the years to honor the operation of this famous train.

(ACL Photo/William E. Griffin, Jr. Collection)

Stung by the Seaboard Air Line Railway's success in 1938 with its diesel powered *Orange Blossom Special* and *Silver Meteor* streamlined train, the ACL quickly moved to counter the competition. The ACL purchased two Electro-Motive Corporation E3-A diesels and introduced its own streamlined passenger train—the *Champion*—that operated during the winter season commencing December 1, 1939 on a daily, 25-hour schedule between New York to Miami via the PRR/RF&P/ACL/FEC route. This retouched publicity photograph depicts the ACL's first diesel—E3-A No. 500—with the *Champion* and its train of new lightweight passenger equipment.

(ACL Photo)

During the years following the Second World War, there was an unprecedented modernization of the ACL's passenger trains as the result of the railroad's dieselization and its acquisition of more than 100 new lightweight cars of all types. Completely re-equipped with new lightweight sleepers, diners and lounge cars, the Florida Special was the train for those travelers for whom the trip was part of the fun and who enjoyed an atmosphere of relaxed elegance. So heavy was the demand for space in the new sleepers that it was not uncommon for there to be several hundred applicants for the train's 60 bedrooms. The ACL's other new streamliners—the *East* and *West Coast Champions*—were also popular with the traveling public. In fact, the *East Coast Champion,* which operated year around as a streamlined all-coach train between the East and Florida, was the railroad's leading passenger moneymaker. The ACL's advertisements such as this one promoted both the new streamlined trains and its smooth new roadbed on the double track route to Florida.

(William E. Griffin, Jr. Collection)

On October 20, 1960, the ACL formally opened its new General Office Building at Jacksonville, Florida. The decision had been made in 1956 to relocate the company's general offices from Wilmington, North Carolina, where they had been located for some 120 years. Situated beside the St. Johns River, the new structure took nearly two years to complete. The building, which serves today as the headquarters for CSX Transportation, is 17 stories high and is shaped roughly in the form of an extended letter "Y". Built almost entirely of concrete and glass, the front and back facades are faced with iridescent turquoise and blue mosaic tile panels, while the end walls are of gray limestone slabs, each weighing 3,000 pounds. The original inside floor space totaled 475,000 square feet.

(ACL Photo)

of the railroad, the Interstate Commerce Commission formally announced that it was rejecting the ACL's proposal to merge the FEC into the Coast Line. However, while the ACL's efforts to acquire the FEC were unsuccessful, it was able to obtain ICC approval to absorb a longtime subsidiary into its system. On December 31, 1959, the Charleston and Western Carolina Railroad was merged into the ACL as its new Western Carolina Division.

The merger of the C&WC into the ACL came as no surprise. It had been controlled by the ACL and operated as an affiliated road since 1898. The real surprise had come a year earlier—in 1958—when Tom Rice and John W. Smith, the president of the Seaboard Air Line Railway, announced that they were studying the benefits to be achieved from the merger of their two railroads. The boards of directors of the ACL and SAL announced their approval of the merger of the railroads in May of 1960 and, on August 18, 1960, the stockholders of both companies approved the merger. However, it would be years before the actual merger could be consummated as the foes of the proposed merger pressed the fight over its approval at the ICC and in the federal court system.

While the merger proceedings were pending, Rice continued to modernize and improve the ACL. By 1963, he had reduced the ACL's operating ratio (ratio of expenses to income) by eight percentage points - from 84 to 76. During the same period—from 1957 to 1963—the ACL's net income climbed by approximately 40 percent.

Under his leadership, the ACL had also achieved a number of firsts in the railroad industry. The ACL was one of the first major railroads in the Southeast to go into the pig-

W. Thomas Rice served as the president of the ACL from 1957 until its merger with the Seaboard Air Line Railway in 1967. He then served as president of the newly formed Seaboard Coast Line Railroad. Unlike his predecessors, Rice had not risen through the ranks of the company to the ACL presidency. He began his career in the railroad industry as a transportation officer with the Pennsylvania Railroad, then established a distinguished record as an Army officer during World War II (eventually he would rise to the rank of major general in the U.S. Army Reserve). Upon his release from active military service in 1946, he joined the RF&P Railroad and served as that company's superintendent of Potomac Yard, general superintendent of transportation and president. His RF&P experience provided Rice with a unique opportunity to gain knowledge of the operations of both the ACL and SAL railroads.

(ACL Photo)

gyback business and the first to run solid piggyback trains between the South and other parts of the country. The ACL also developed and introduced a number of specialized freight cars, such as giant woodchip cars and the so-called "Whopper Hopper", each tailored to specific industry requirements. In the engineering area, the ACL built the first prestressed concrete railroad

bridges in the country and was among the first to test the use of prestressed concrete ties in its tracks. The ACL also continued to promote its passenger service and offered a full range of amenities and innovations, such as on-board movies, fashion shows, hostess service, telephones and television. The ACL also installed the railroad industry's first "on-line-real-time" data processing system during the period between 1964 and 1966.

Early in 1967, the ACL issued the 133rd Annual Report to its stockholders. This historic report not only told the story in detail of the year 1966, it also recorded the railroad's last full year of existence. By any measure, the ACL's last year was a very good one.

Gross ton-miles per freight train reached an all-time high, and the operating ratio of 76 was the best since 1944. Freight revenues also climbed to a record high and the Florida Special began its 79th season in December of 1966 as the most popular train running between New York and Miami. The dividend of $4.00 per share on earnings of $8.20 per share represented the largest return to the owners in the history of the Company.

In April of 1967, the ACL and SAL received the long awaited news that their merger proposal had finally been approved by the Supreme Court of the United States. The merger had originally been approved by the Interstate Commerce Commission in orders

As evidenced by its experiment with the R-1 Class 4-8-4 steam engines purchased in 1938, the ACL did not immediately embrace the new diesel-electric locomotives. However, the ACL's R-1 break-in problems and costly maintenance compared with the remarkable success of the SAL's diesel-powered *Silver Meteor* won over the Coast Line management. Within five years, the ACL had acquired more than 100 diesel-electric locomotives for both yard and road service. These diesel locomotives proved so successful that by the 1952 the ACL had almost completely replaced its steam motive power with new diesels. Only 11 steam locomotives remained on the roster to serve two small branch lines. The last steam locomotives on the ACL were retired in 1955. In a photo symbolic of steam's demise, the victor—in the form of ACL first generation F and GP diesels—haul a "funeral train" of vanquished ACL steam locomotives to be scrapped.

(ACL Photo)

dated December 2, 1963 and March 4, 1964. However, opponents of the merger took the matter into federal court with the case reaching the U. S. Supreme Court twice on appeals. The Supreme Court's decision on April 10, 1967, upholding a lower court's approval of the merger, finally cleared the way for the consolidation of the two railroads.

The merger was consummated on July 1, 1967, creating the new Seaboard Coast Line Railroad. John W. Smith, President of the SAL, was elected to serve as Chairman of the Board and Tom Rice was elected to serve as President of the merged company. Both of the original companies had sought the same

destination when their routes were laid out - access to the Roanoke River and the opportunity to provide transportation for the output of the farms, mills and mines situated on the upper reaches of the river. The creation of the new Seaboard Coast Line Railroad brought an end to the long-standing rivalry between the Coast Line and the Seaboard and to the proud histories of each railroad. However, neither the new company nor the passage of time has dimmed the glorious history or the fond memories of the old Atlantic Coast Line Railroad - The Standard Railroad of the South.

In 1958, the officers of the ACL and SAL announced that the longtime competitors had agreed to study the possible advantages of merging their two systems. The proposed plan of merger was approved in 1960 but its consummation was delayed until 1967 as opponents fought the merger in the federal court system. The two companies were finally merged on July 1, 1967 forming the new Seaboard Coast Line Railroad. In one of many publicity photographs to celebrate the merger, ACL president Tom Rice (to the right) prepares to cut a cake topped by "Miss Seaboard Coast Line". To the left in the photo is former SAL president John W. Smith, who was named Chairman of the Board of the new SCL. Rice was named president of the new company. Behind Rice in the photo is Prime F. Osborn, Vice President - Law and also a member of the Board of the new SCL Railroad.

(SCL Photo)

Under the direction of Champ Davis, the ACL almost completely rebuilt and transformed itself in the period between 1938 and 1952. Its physical rehabilitation program involved the expenditure of more than $258 million in gross additions and improvements to roadway and equipment. A top priority, which began in 1943, was the replacement of 100-lb. rail on the double track main line between Richmond and Jacksonville with 131-lb. (later 132-lb.) rail. This project was completed early in 1950. For important secondary main lines, but of lesser traffic density, a standard of 115-lb. section rail was adopted. Improvement of the roadway continued under Tom Rice. In 1958, the ACL began to install 132-lb. welded rail on its main line. Regular lengths of the existing main line were taken up, welded together and installed as relay rail on branch lines. By 1966, this relay rail was being welded at a plant at Rocky Mount and was hauled to the installation site on special 29-car rail trains. By the end of 1966, the ACL had installed more than 400 miles of continuous welded rail on its lines. In this scene, a versatile crane, equipped with both flanged steel and rubber wheels, positions a quarter-mile length of rail on the crossties and tie plates. The rail is then field-welded to create continuous miles of welded track. The ACL used many such cranes in its modern rail laying programs.

(ACL Photo)

THE BALDWIN LOCOMOTIVE WORKS.

Steam Locomotives: Switchers

The standard switch engine on the ACL for many years were the 0-6-0 locomotives. The ACL owned about 175 such locomotives in the Classes E through E-13, some joining the system from predecessor companies. Built in 1904 by Baldwin for the ACL, No. 176 was one of sixty-five E-4 Class 0-6-0's numbered in the series 126 to 190. The locomotive is at Waycross, Georgia on April 29, 1948.

(James Bowie Photo/David W. Salter Collection)

Top Left: This peculiar looking locomotive is one of six four-wheeled switchers that were built by Baldwin for ACL predecessor companies between 1891 and 1912. Numbered 430-435, the switchers were "dummy" type locomotives with enclosed engines for noiseless operation on city streets. These locomotives were later renumbered as 1430-1435. The 435, shown here, was rebuilt in 1914 with the box cab removed and closed out its career on the ACL as a saddle-tank shop switcher at Rocky Mount.

(Baldwin Photo)

Bottom Left: ACL 0-4-0 switcher No. 1434, former dummy engine No. 434, is shown switching the streets of Montgomery, Alabama on September 15, 1939. This locomotive's "dummy" box cab was also removed in 1914 and it was equipped with a tender for operation in Montgomery as an 0-4-0 switch engine.

(Bruce R. Meyer Collection)

ACL Class E 0-6-0 switcher No. 106 poses with its crew at Waycross, Georgia on March 3, 1930. The locomotive had 18"x24" cylinders, 50" drive wheels and weighed 88,000 pounds. The 106 was retired and scrapped three years after this photograph was taken.

(All: ACL Photo)

Another view of E-11 Class 0-6-0 switcher No. 1127 shifting cars at Wilmington. This view shows the details of the locomotive's tender including the ACL herald.

Right: Class E-11 0-6-0 switcher No. 1127 pulls forward to clear the switch while working the ladder track at the Wilmington, North Carolina yard. Built by Baldwin in 1916, 1127 and its sister locomotive No. 1126, were superheated with piston valve cylinders and Southern valve gear. They were the ACL's first superheated switchers and worked at various locations on the system until retired in the early-1950s.

A head-on view of Class E-14 No. 1200 shows the locomotive's footboards and the headlight repositioned to the center of the smokebox. These locomotives weighed over 215,000 pounds and dwarfed the 0-6-0 shifters in both size and performance.

(ACL Photo)

Top: Heavy traffic generated by World War I convinced the ACL that it needed a more powerful switch locomotive for its major terminals. Between 1923 and 1926, Baldwin delivered thirty-five superheated, 51" eight-drive wheel locomotives, with 25"x 28" piston valve cylinders and Walschaert valve gear. These locomotives were numbered 1200-1234 and assigned as Class E-14. No. 1217 is shown in an early photo prior to the relocation of its headlight to the center of the smokebox.

(ACL Photo)

Center: Except for its Walschaert valve gear, the E-14 0-8-0's were very similar in design to the USRA standard eight wheel switchers. Carrying over 185 pounds of steam pressure per square inch, they developed a starting effort of 53,960 pounds with an adhesion ratio of 1 to 3.96. The E-14 tender was the conventional rectangular type with a capacity of 16 tons of coal and 8,000 gallons of water, carried on two four-wheel trucks of the Andrews type. ACL E-14 No. 1230 is shifting at Hot Springs, Florida in 1950.

(George A. Pettengill, Jr. Photo/C. K. Marsh, Jr. Collection)

Bottom: Several 0-6-0 and 0-8-0 locomotives were added to the roster of the ACL when it acquired the Atlanta, Birmingham and Coast Railroad in 1946. The motive power of the AB&C was renumbered to the ACL 7000 series. ACL Class AS-2 0-8-0 No. 7031 (formerly AB&C No. 31) is shown in yard service at Atlanta, Georgia on January 15, 1948.

(Bruce R. Meyer Collection)

From the earliest days of American railroading, the standard motive power for both passenger and freight service on the ACL, as well as on the other roads, was the 4-4-0 or "American" type of locomotive. Noted for their high speed capabilities, most of the ACL 4-4-0's were built during the 1870s or 1880s and remained in active service until the late 1920s. ACL No. 61, an F class 4-4-0 built by Baldwin in 1881, is shown in passenger service at Rocky Mount, North Carolina in May of 1924.

(Joseph Lavelle Photo/Harold K. Vollrath Collection)

The Baldwin Locomotive Works introduced the Columbia, or 2-4-2 type of steam locomotive, at the 1893 World's Columbian Exposition in Chicago. Designed for high-speed passenger service, these locomotives interested ACL officials who were then in the market for a new type of motive power that could replace the 4-4-0 locomotives by achieving higher steaming capacity without exceeding the weight limits that could be carried on four drive wheels. ACL No. 154, shown here in a Baldwin builder photograph, was one of two 2-4-2 locomotives purchased by the ACL in 1895.

(Baldwin Locomotive Works/ACL Photo)

In tests conducted between 1895 and 1897, the ACL found that the larger boilers of the 4-4-2 type of locomotive provided superior steaming capability to that of the 2-4-2 s. Hence, the ACL opted for the 4-4-2 s instead of the 2-4-2 s for its high speed passenger service. The ACL's only two 2-4-2 locomotives were numbered 153 and 154, later renumbered 206 and 207, and finally ended their careers as Nos. 93 and 94 on branch line passenger trains. With the exception of its headlight, No. 94 (former No. 154)—shown here on a turntable in the early-1930s—reveals few modifications from its as-delivered appearance. Both of the ACL 2-4-2's were retired and scrapped in 1934.

(ACL Photo)

In the evolution of the steam locomotive, the 2-6-0 or Mogul type, became the standard freight engine by the 1890s for many railroads. Heavy grades between Sanford and Port Tampa dictated that the Plant System own over 60 of these types of engines. However, the Moguls were not as prominent on the ACL System because of its moderate ruling grades. Mogul No. 670 (former 415) was one of two such locomotives built by Baldwin for high speed freight service on the ACL's Norfolk and Carolina Railroad in 1896. The locomotive is shown on the storage line at Waycross, Georgia in May of 1924. It was retired and scrapped in 1933.

(Joseph Lavelle Photo/Harold K. Vollrath Collection)

In 1898, the ACL System ordered six "Tenwheeler" 4-6-0 type locomotive from the Baldwin Locomotive Works. They were distributed among the various roads of the system and it was soon found that their 19"x 26" cylinders, 63-inch drivers and 22,800 pounds of tractive effort made them ideal locomotives for use in both passenger and freight service. As reported by Richard E. Prince in his book, *Atlantic Coast Line Railroad Steam Locomotives, Ships and History*, these locomotives were affectionately called "Copper Heads" on the ACL because of the brightly polished crown of copper on the top of their smokestacks. The original "Copper Heads" were designated as the K Class by ACL and most of the locomotives were built by the Baldwin Locomotive Works. The original "Copper Head" stack is noticeable in this builder photograph of No. 326, which was one of six "Copper Heads" built by the Richmond Locomotive and Machine Works.

(American Locomotive Company/ACL Photo)

K-15 Class tenwheeler No. 1031 is shown during its lay over at Parmele, North Carolina on July 30, 1959 while working the ACL's old Washington and Vandemere line. The 1031 was built by Baldwin for the ACL in 1913. This locomotive operated on the East Carolina Railroad beginning in 1955 and was then donated by the ACL in 1959 to the town of Florence, South Carolina.

(J. I. Kelly Photo

Bottom: K-16 Class tenwheeler No. 1045, photographed at Montgomery, Alabama in March of 1939 was one-of-a-kind locomotive. It was built in 1922 by the Baldwin Locomotive Works as an experimental engine for the ACL's Motive Power Department. With 23" x 26" piston valve type cylinders, this superheated locomotive developed 37,200 pounds of tractive effort, it was the most powerful tenwheeler and was even slightly more powerful than the ACL's P-4 Pacifics. However, the Class P-5-B Pacifics ultimately proved to be better suited to the ACL's needs and the 1045 was the last tenwheeler purchased by the railroad.

(Harold K. Vollrath Collection)

The original "Copper Head" smokestack was later replaced on the tenwheelers by one with the standard cast iron tapered design. The tenwheelers were also renumbered with those in freight service assigned numbers in the 300, 900 and 1000 series. Passenger service locomotives were assigned numbers in the 200 series. K-6 Class tenwheeler No. 904, shown here with a tapered stack, was one of a group of tenwheelers built by Baldwin between 1904 and 1906 for freight service on the ACL. The K-6 tenwheelers, numbered 351-399 and 900-909, had 20"x26" cylinders, 63" drive wheels and exerted 25,900 pounds of tractive effort. The 904 is in immaculate condition after having been turned out of the Tampa, Florida shops following modification with superheaters.

(ACL Photo)

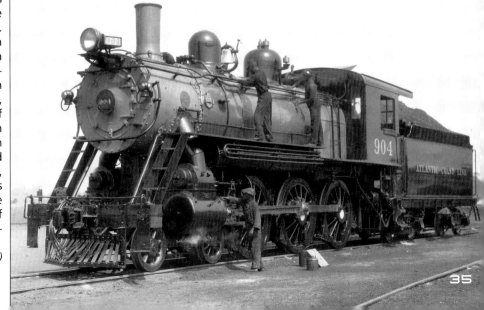

Top: In addition to its own large roster of ten-wheelers, a number of these locomotives came to the ACL from its predecessor and acquired roads. No. 210 is a K-9 Class tenwheeler built by Baldwin in 1900 for the Savannah, Florida and Western Railway of the Plant System. With 73" drivers and 21,240 pounds of tractive effort, the K-9 Class engines were the fastest tenwheelers on the ACL. This particular locomotive set an unofficial speed record of 120 miles per hour on March 1, 1901 on a five-mile stretch of track between Screven and Satilla, Georgia, while competing for a mail contract.
(Both: ACL Photo)

Bottom: The last tenwheelers acquired by the ACL were the seventeen locomotives that came in 1946 with the purchase of the Atlanta, Birmingham and Coast Railroad. All numbered in the 7100 series, the lighter engines were designated at the AW-1 and AW-2 classes, while the heavier engines were classified as the AW-3 and AW-4. Class AW-4 No. 7124, shown here in a retouched ACL company photograph, was superheated with piston valve cylinders, had 67" drivers and developed a tractive effort of 37,580 pounds.

Unlike many railroads, the ACL had a small roster of 2-8-0, or Consolidation type steam loco-motives. The first such locomotives came to the ACL from the Alabama Midland Railway of the Plant System. Predominantly used in slow speed heavy freight service, the 2-8-0's (num-bered 530-533) were ideally suited for the coal and lumber traffic handled by that road between Dothan and Montgomery, Alabama and thence from Montgomery to Florida and southern Georgia. Alabama Midland Railway No. 532 was built by Baldwin in 1901 and was renumbered ACL L Class No. 702.

(Baldwin Locomotive Works/ACL Photo)

The Plant System's four 2-8-0's were designated the ACL L Class and renumbered 700-703 in 1903. The ACL then acquired sixteen new Consolidations (Nos. 704-720) from Baldwin between 1903 and 1911. These L-1 and L-2 engines had generally similar specifications to the L Class, but were slightly heavier locomotives. These locomotives primarily worked in the Montgomery District until replaced by the Mikado locomotives. Thereafter, they were used in local freight service throughout the system. L-1 Class 2-8-0 No. 716 is shown in local freight service at Richmond, Virginia in June of 1948.

(Harold K. Vollrath Collection)

Three of the L-1 Class 2-8-0's (Nos. 714-716) were rebuilt with superheaters and modern piston valve steam chests. These locomotives were designated as the Class L-1-S and were renumbered 2714-2716. This historic photograph of No. 2715 from the files of the ACL is captioned "the last steam engine operating at Thomasville, Georgia."

(ACL Photo)

Bottom Left: The ACL inherited seventeen Mikados from the Atlanta, Birmingham and Coast Railroad in 1946 and they were designated as Class AK-1 (Nos. 7205, 7208 and 7209), AK-2 (7225-7235) and AK-3 (7301-7302). Class AK-1 No. 7208 was photographed rolling a southbound local freight at an estimated 45 mph south of Cordele, Georgia on April 24, 1948.

(David W. Salter Photo)

Top Left: While the undulating profile of the Seaboard Air Line Railway's inland route made the Mikado steam locomotive a standard for that railroad's freight motive power, the ACL had little need for such engines on its flat coastal main line south of Richmond, Virginia. Prior to its 1946 acquisition of the AB&C Railroad, the ACL owned only thirty-nine Mikado, or 2-8-2 type locomotives, which were primarily assigned to the Southern Division. The first ACL Mikado locomotives were designated as Class M and were delivered by Baldwin in 1911 as Nos. 800-819. They were later reclassified as Class M-S when modified with superheaters and modernized steam chests. The ACL purchased ten heavier Mikado locomotives (designated Class M-2 and numbered 820-829) to handle the coal traffic in the Montgomery District during the first World War. M-2 2-8-2 No. 822 blows off steam as it pulls away from the engine house after servicing for its next trip.

(ACL Photo)

In 1923, Baldwin delivered ten final 2-8-2's to the ACL, also designated as M-2 and numbered 830-839. With 27"x 30" cylinders, 64" drivers and a tractive effort of 58,000 pounds, the M-2 Mikado locomotives were the most powerful steam locomotives at that

time. M-2 No. 830 looks every bit of its 287,700 pounds as its awaits the next call to service at Tampa, Florida in April of 1948. They were also every Fireman s nightmare as they were delivered as hand-fired engines from Baldwin and remained that way for many years. Eventually, they were equipped with Standard HT stokers. These locomotives worked the coal districts of Montgomery and the central hills of Florida into Tampa. The M Class 2-8-2's also worked the phosphate districts of Florida. All of the ACL 2-8-2's were retired in the early 1950s.

(James Bowie Photo/Harold K. Vollrath Collection)

In 1917, a group of locomotives with a 2-10-0 type wheel arrangement that had been built by both the Baldwin and American locomotive works for Czarist Russia could not be delivered account the Bolshevik revolution. The locomotives were returned to their builders and were then assigned to various American railroads by the United States Railroad Administration that had taken over operation of the railroads during the first World War. Many of these locomotives, called "Decapods" or "Russian Decapods", were subsequently returned to the Government after the war. However, the locomotives performance impressed the ACL's motive power department and it acquired ten of the engines for local freight service. When photographed at Richmond, Virginia in May of 1938, Decapod No. 8005 was being used in transfer service from ACL's Clopton Yard to the RF&P s Acca Yard.

(W. H. Thrall Photo/Harold K. Vollrath Collection)

The ACL's Decapods were numbered 8000-8009 and originally were assigned as the S Class. In later years they were reclassified as the O Class. They were equipped with a Schmidt superheater, had 25"x28" cylinders, 52 inch drivers and were used in local freight and branch line service throughout the ACL's system. S Class No. 8009 is at Montgomery, Alabama in July of 1935.

(Harold K. Vollrath Collection)

Left: While the Q-1 2-10-2s were assigned to heavy freight service on the ACL's Western and Southern Divisions, some of the locomotives were equipped with automatic train control for operation on the main line into Acca Yard at Richmond. Photographer Bob Crockett captured on film this operation of Q-1 No. 2019 with an Extra-Northbound Freight at Petersburg, Virginia in April of 1943. Bob photographed the train from "BX" Tower after it had departed ACL's Collier Yard en route to Richmond, Virginia. When delivered by Baldwin, the Q-1's were equipped with 63" drive wheels and were originally restricted to a maximum speed of 30 m.p.h. However, as the maximum speed was increased in later years to meet the needs of the service, it was discovered that it was impossible to provide within the small diameter of the main driving wheels, the necessary counterweights to properly balance the revolving weights on the main crank pin and the weights due to the reciprocating parts. At increased speeds, the unbalanced weight of the locomotive resulted in severe damage to the track and road bed. To resolve this problem, the original spoke type main drive wheel centers were replaced with Baldwin disc design wheel centers in 1938.

(Robert S. Crockett Photo)

The most powerful steam engines to ever operate on the ACL were the Q-1 Class 2-10-2 "Santa Fe" type locomotive. Twenty of these behemoths, numbered 2000-2019, were built for the ACL by the Baldwin Locomotive Works in 1925. Developing a maximum starting tractive force of 81,600 pounds, they were used exclusively for heavy freight service where sustained power was required and where the contour of the track was such as to permit the use of a long wheel-base locomotive. The name "Santa Fe" was derived from the fact that locomotives of this wheel arrangement were first used on the Atchison, Topeka and Santa Fe Railroad. ACL Q-1 Class 2-10-2 No. 2015 is at Thomasville, Georgia in 1930.

(ACL Photo)

Bottom Left: Q-1 No. 2001 is at the Waycross, Georgia on March 31, 1930. The Q-1's tender, clearly shown in this photograph, was of the cylindrical Vanderbilt tank type with a coal capacity of sixteen tons and boiler feed water capacity of 12,000 gallons. The total working weight of the engine and tender was 613,000 pounds. To increase the working distance between stops for boiler water, an auxiliary tender was converted from a standard tank car for service with some of these engines. The Duplex D-1 stoker was installed by Baldwin, making the Q-1's the ACL's first stoker-fired locomotives. Standard HT stokers were subsequently installed on the engines.

(ACL Photo)

Left: As train weights increased after the first World War because of new steel passenger equipment and longer freight trains, the ACL discovered that even its easy ruling grade between Richmond and Jacksonville required more power for high speed operations than could be supplied by the 4-6-0's. The ACL's Mechanical Department was looking for a dual purpose engine that could handle trains of either high speed main line passenger or freight service. It would eventually find that engine in the 4-6-2 Pacific type locomotive. The Plant System had been experimenting with a Pacific type locomotive since 1902. However, those Pacifics proved to be unsatisfactory and were finally converted to 4-6-0's. The first ACL System Pacifics were fifteen P Class 4-6-2's (Nos. 260-274) delivered by Baldwin in 1911. These engines had 72" drive wheels and were designed for main line passenger service. They were an immediate success and the following year, ACL ordered twelve more Pacifics from Baldwin. These locomotives, the P-1 Class numbered 275-286, had 73" drivers and were delivered with superheaters and new style cylinders cast with piston valve steam chest. Passenger service P-1 Class 4-6-2 No. 276 is on ready track at Waycross, Georgia on March 31, 1930.

Right: The first 4-6-2s purchased by the ACL for freight service were the P-2 Class Pacifics numbered 287-297. Built by Baldwin in 1913, they had smaller 64" drive wheels but developed about 5,000 more pounds of tractive effort than the P-1

passenger service Pacifics. The P-2's were renumbered 400-410 in 1914 and, while suitable for heavy passenger service, they performed best in freight service. The ACL's first true dual-purpose Pacifics were the Class P-3 4-6-2's (Nos. 411-455) delivered by Baldwin in 1914. An immaculately maintained P-3 No. 433 is shown on the ready track at Waycross, Georgia on March 31, 1930. These locomotives had 69" drive wheels and developed 33,400 pound of tractive effort with 200 pounds of steam pressure. Their outstanding performance in both passenger and freight service convinced the ACL's Mechanical Department that Pacific locomotives could successfully operate in dual service on the main line between Richmond and Jacksonville.

(Both: ACL Photo)

Top Left: Three more 2-10-2 locomotives were added to the ACL's roster after the acquisition of the AB&C Railroad. Assigned the class designation AF-1, the locomotives were numbered 7401-7403. The former AB&C 2-10-2's, such as No. 7403 at Bellwood Yard in Atlanta, Georgia in August of 1948, were smaller than the ACL's Q-1 type engines. They were equipped with disc-type main drivers and Elesco type feedwater heaters were mounted in front of the smokestack.
Bottom Left: Just getting underway from Atlanta, Georgia, AF-1 Class 2-10-2 No. 7403 (former AB&C No. 403) rounds the sweeping curve at Maddox Park with a southbound freight in June of 1948. Photographer David Salter felt that the AB&C did a magnificent job in rebuilding its three 2-10-2's and they became one of his favorite AB&C/ACL locomotives.

(Both: David W. Salter Photo)

Top Left: The ACL obtained a group of more powerful dual-service 4-6-2's in 1917-1918, when Baldwin delivered twenty-seven Class P-4 Pacifics numbered 456-482. Like their predecessors, these superheated engines had 69" drive wheels and 23" x 28" cylinders, but were heavier and developed over 3,000 pounds more tractive effort than the P-3's. In this photo, P-4 No. 475 gets under way with a freight train at Lakeland, Florida in May of 1949. Note the Spanish Moss hanging from the nearby tree and the friendly wave from the "hobo" who is catching a free ride from the ACL on this trip in the ventilated boxcar behind the engine.

(Harold K. Vollrath Photo)

Bottom Left: While they also operated in fast freight service, from 1919 until 1938, the mainstay of the ACL's main line passenger service were the Class P-5-A locomotives in the number series 1500-1569. The first 45 of these locomotives were built in 1918 by the American Locomotive Company under the direction of the United States Railroad Administration. They were delivered as Class P-5 Nos. 493-502, but were soon renumbered in the 1500 series and reclassified at the P-5-A. Twenty-five more of these Pacifics were ordered from the American Locomotive Company in 1920. The diameter of the drive wheels was 73" and with 200 pounds of steam pressure per square inch and 25" x 28" cylinders, the 1500's developed a starting effort of 40,750 pounds with a ratio of adhesion of 4.12 to 4.28. The grate area of the firebox was 66.7 square feet which afforded ample heating pressure on long runs at high speed. The total heating surface was 3,191 square feet. In this splendid view, P-5-A No. 1510 is shown departing Atlanta, Georgia with a southbound freight on October 19, 1946.

(R. D. Sharpless, Jr. Photo/David W. Salter Collection)

P-5-A 4-6-2's were equipped with Baker valve gear and Franklin Radial Buffers between the engine and tender, which improved the quality of the ride for the engine crew and lessened the wear on the driving wheel flanges and track The tenders were of the conventional rectangular type with a carrying capacity of 16 tons of coal and 10,000 gallons of water. In later years, the engines were improved with the addition of stokers and feedwater heaters. To the joy of their firemen, the tenders of the 1500's were also equipped with air-operated coal pushers. P-5-A No. 1527 sports painted wheel tires and running boards as well as double-lined striping in this view taken at Fitzgerald, Georgia in June of 1949.

(Harold K. Vollrath Collection)

All of the ACL's 1500-series Pacifics were retired between 1949 and 1952. However, one of these locomotives, No. 1504, was preserved by the company and for many years was a static display on the grounds of the ACL's General Office Building in Jacksonville, Florida. It was subsequently moved to the grounds of the Prime Osborn Convention Center (formerly Jacksonville Union Terminal) where it serves as a constant reminder of the glory days of steam on the ACL. In this splendid in-service view of the 1504, its engine crew waits for the signal from their Conductor to high ball their passenger train from St. Petersburg, Florida in 1946.

(George W. Pettengill, Jr. Photo/C. K. Marsh, Jr. Collection)

Bottom Left: While the 1500-series Pacific excelled in main line passenger service, it was unable to achieve the optimum efficiencies in freight operations that were desired by the ACL. The mechanical engineers at the ACL and at the Baldwin Locomotive Works went back to the drawing table and the result was the creation of the P-5-B Pacific. Numbered 1600-1764 and delivered by Baldwin between 1922 and 1926, these locomotives became the ideal engine for either passenger or fast freight service. In general, they resembled the Class P-5-A Pacifics, but had 69" drivers instead of 73" and carried 210 pounds steam pressure instead of 200 pounds. With the same grate and heating surface as the P-5-A Class but with a higher steam pressure, they developed a starting tractive effort of 45,275 pounds, or an increase of 4,525 pounds. This splendid view of P-5-B No. 1718 was taken as the locomotive departed East Albany, Georgia with an eastbound extra freight on December 28, 1947.

(George B. Mock, Jr. Photo/David W. Salter)

Doing what a P-5-A Pacific did best, No. 1560 rolls a passenger train of heavy weight equipment through the semaphore signals on the stretch of main line double track at Mile Post 290.4, near Florence, South Carolina. The passenger trains that operated between Richmond and Jacksonville were long, and the schedules fast, but the "high stepping" 1500-series 4-6-2 were equal to the job.

(ACL Photo)

Left: While the Class P-5-B Pacific was designed, and did serve as a true dual-service locomotive, it soon became the ACL's standard main line freight locomotive. Thus, the ACL had the unique distinction among American railroads of operating both its main line passenger and freight trains with the Pacific type steam locomotive. In this view, P-5-B No. 1608 handles a southbound freight at Ben Hill, Georgia in July of 1949. The first 70 of the 1600's, were equipped with Walschaert Valve Gear and Woodward engine trucks. Nos. 1600-1669 had Cole-Scoville trailer trucks, while Nos. 1670-1764 had Delta trailer trucks. Their tenders were similar to those of the P-5-A Class Pacifics and were equipped with coal-pushers. The engines were equipped with non-lifting injectors that enabled crews to make longer runs before stopping for water. The locomotives were later improved with stokers, feedwater heaters and disc-type drivers.

(David W. Salter Photo)

Left: A final group of fourteen Pacific locomotives were added to the ACL s roster in 1946 from the AB&C Railroad. The eleven AB&C light Pacifics, which weighed less than the smallest of the ACL s own 4-6-2 s, became ACL Class AJ-1 and were numbered in the 7000-series. Two AB&C heavy Pacifics became ACL Class AJ-2 and were numbered 7153 and 7175. Both groups of engines had an interesting ancestry. The light Pacifics had been acquired by the AB&C from the Florida East Coast Railroad. The AB&C had acquired the two heavy 4-6-2's from the Great Northern Railway. Class AJ-1 Pacific No. 7073 shows off its new ACL paint scheme in the Company portrait.

(ACL Photo)

P-5-B Class 4-6-2 No. 1683 passes "GY" Tower and weaves its way through the crossovers on the line leading to Tampa Union Station with a long passenger train of heavy weight equipment. Even though it was considered the standard main line freight locomotive, the P-5-B's could make the fast running times required of the heavy passenger trains. The maximum speed limit for P-5-B's with disc-type drive wheels was set at 75 m.p.h.

(ACL Photo)

In its first year of service after the acquisition of the AB&C by the ACL, Class AJ-1 4-6-2 No. 7075 rolls a passenger train at Atlanta, Georgia on October 16, 1946. Note the interesting paint scheme of the train's heavy weight passenger equipment. The ex-AB&C Pacifics stayed on their former home rails after the acquisition and handled trains over what had become the Western Division of the ACL.

(Bruce R. Meyer Collection)

Because of heavy freight and passenger traffic to the west coast of Florida during World War II, the ACL purchased five Mountain, or 4-8-2, type locomotives from the Delaware, Lackawanna and Western Railroad in 1943. Designated as Class J-1 by the ACL, they retained their Lackawanna road numbers (1401-1405) as ACL locomotives. These locomotives were primarily assigned to work in passenger service handling the Southland from Tampa, Florida to Albany, Georgia but also worked on

freight trains from Tampa and on passenger runs that operated north of Jacksonville. It's tender fully loaded with coal, Class J-1 4-8-2 No. 1404 is at the Albany, Georgia engine terminal ready for a run to Tampa in March of 1949.

(Harold K. Vollrath Collection)

Steam Locomotives: 4-6-2, 4-8-2

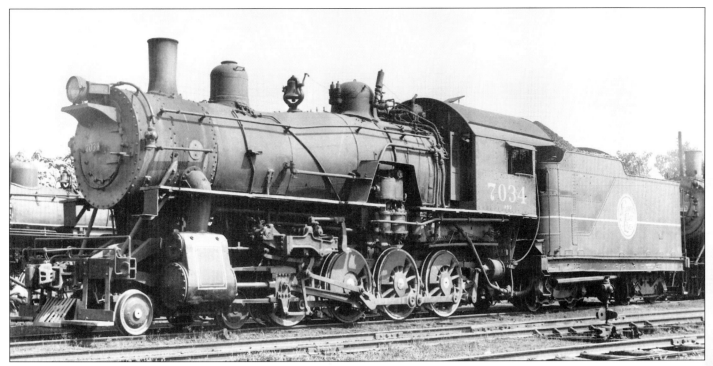

Locomotive No. 7034 was a one-of-a-kind locomotive on the ACL—the only Mastodon 4-8-0 type engine ever owned by the railroad. No. 7034 also came to the ACL from the AB&C in 1946. It was designated Class AS-3 by the ACL and was used as a yard engine at Birmingham, Alabama until retired and scrapped in 1949. The engine had originally been built by Baldwin for the Norfolk and Western in 1906 and was purchased by the AB&C from the High Point, Thomasville and Denton Railroad. It is seen here while working at Birmingham in September of 1946.

(Harold K. Vollrath Collection)

The AB&C Railroad also owned two 4-8-2 Mountain locomotives that had been acquired from the Florida East Coast Railroad for operation on the *Dixieland* winter tourist train. They became ACL Class AM-1 and were renumbered 7351 and 7372. They were lighter than the J-1 Class Mountains and developed only 46, 920 pounds of tractive effort compared to 61,135 pounds developed by the J-1's. With their 72" drive wheels, they were used primarily in passenger service. AM-1 No. 7372 is shown at Fitzgerald, Georgia in July of 1948.

(John B. Allen Photo/Harold K. Vollrath Collection)

With an almost clear stack, AM-1 4-8-2 No. 7372 rolls past with a short northbound freight near Ben Hill, Georgia on May 9, 1948.
(Richard O. Sharpless Photo/David W. Salter)

The J-1 Class Mountains had 28"x30" cylinders, 69" drive wheels and developed a tractive effort of 61,135 pounds with 210 pounds of steam pressure. The were equipped with stokers, feedwater heaters and Franklin driving box lubricators. Mountain No. 1403 rides the turntable at Jacksonville, Florida surrounded by the ACL's new E6A diesel locomotives. All of the ACL's 4-8-2's would be retired and scrapped in 1951 and 1952.

(ACL Photo)

As the country's economy recovered from the Great Depression during the late-1930s, the Florida tourist travel returned to the railroads. This business had always been handled by long trains of heavyweight cars operated on fast schedules and when more cars were added to accommodate the increased patronage it was necessary to doublehead the 1500-series Pacifics to take care of the tonnage. While the ACL's chief competitor, the Seaboard Air Line Railway, was experimenting with new diesel powered locomotives to meet its motive power requirements on the Florida trains, the ACL once again turned to the mechanical engineers at Baldwin Locomotive Works to develop a more powerful and efficient steam locomotive. Baldwin's answer would be twelve R-1 Class 4-8-4—the most modern steam locomotives ever owned by the ACL. Numbered 1800-1811, these locomotives were delivered in 1938. The first of the R-1's, No. 1800, poses for the ACL's company photographer at Waycross, Georgia.

(ACL Photo)

Steam Locomotives: 4-8-4

The R-1's were delivered with 27"x30" cylinders, 80" disc type drive wheels and developed 63,900 pounds of tractive effort with 275 pounds of steam pressure. The locomotives were built on a one-piece bed frame cast connected with the cylinders and main reservoirs. The engine weighed a massive 460,270 pounds and dwarfed the ACL's Pacifics that were operating the Richmond/Jacksonville passenger trains. The R-1's, such as No. 1800, shown here in another company photo, contained many features that were being incorporated into the design of modern steam locomotives by the late-1930s. In addition to their disc-type drivers, that were mounted on axles running on roller bearings, the firebox was equipped with thermic syphons and the engine was superheated and outfitted with a Standard HT stoker.

(ACL Photo)

One of the most distinctive features of the R-1 4-8-4 locomotive was its massive tender. Supported by two eight-wheel trucks, the R-1's tender held 27 tons of coal and 24,000 gallons of water. A fully loaded tender weighed 435,500 pounds making for a total engine weight of nearly 900,000 pounds. The coal and water carried by its colossal tender allowed the R-1's to handle passenger trains without change between Richmond and Jacksonville. The paint scheme of the tender—as well as that of the locomotive—was also unique to the R-1's. The lower portions of the engine and tender were painted black, while the engine's boiler jacket was left unpainted and the cab sides and upper half of the tender were painted a metallic gray. The R-1's were also the first ACL steam locomotive to display the company's herald on its tender. The massive tender and its paint scheme are featured in this rear view of the R-1 No. 1808. Some of the R-1 tenders actually served behind steam for another five years after the end of ACL steam. They were sold to the Norfolk and Western in 1953, sent through Roanoke Shops and placed behind the 1927-built Class Y4 2-8-8-2's (Nos. 2080-89) and soldiered on through to their retirement in the first half of 1958.

(ACL Photo)

R-1 Class 4-8-4 No. 1805 was photographed during a station stop at Charleston, South Carolina with the *Havana Special's* train of heavyweight equipment. With a maximum operating speed of 90 m.p.h. (after correction for initial counterbalancing problems), the R-1's could handle a train of 20 standard heavy weight cars on the schedule of the fastest passenger runs. They were regularly assigned to the Havana Special and also handled the seasonal *Florida Special, Vacationer* and *Miamian.*

(ACL Photo)

As steam locomotives were progressively bumped from the main line passenger assignments by the arrival of the ACL's new E-unit diesel locomotives, the R-1 4-8-4's were increasing used in freight service. R-1 No. 1801 is flying the white flags of an extra freight near Richmond, Virginia in the waning days of its service on the ACL. The 1801 was retired in June of 1952 and all of these magnificent locomotives were removed from active service by December of that year.

(H. Reid Photo)

DIESEL LOCOMOTIVES

To replace steam locomotives on its freight trains, the ACL selected the FT diesel-electrics that were developed by the Electro-Motive Division of General Motors Corporation. As originally purchased in 1943, the loco-motives were delivered in sets of two 2700-horsepower units. Each 2700-horsepower unit was composed of one "A" 1350-horsepower section and one "B" 1350-horsepower section. When the two units were coupled back to back and operated together in an A-B-B-A configuration, they developed a combined 5400-horsepower. Between 1943-1944, the ACL purchased twenty-four sets of EMC FT A-B units with the FT "A" units assigned road numbers 300-323 and the FT "B" units numbered 300-B to 323-B. The first FT set, "A" unit No. 300 and "B" unit No. 300-B, are shown in their original paint scheme shortly after their arrival in 1943.

(ACL Photo)

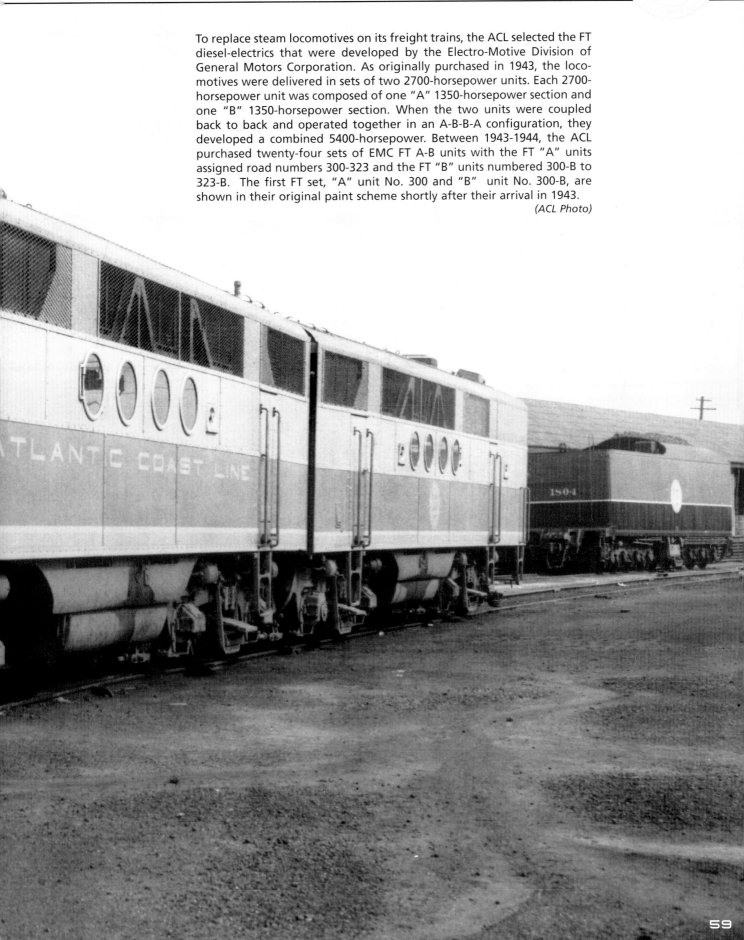

Baldwin VO-1000 No. 18 (formerly No. 623) is shown in the later ACL black and yellow paint scheme while in yard service at Lakeland, Florida in 1966. The ACL owned nine VO-1000 type switchers initially numbered variously from 606 to 623 and renumbered 10-18 in 1955. All except No. 17 were repowered between 1959 and 1961 with EMD engines to 1200-horsepower.

(Kenneth M. Ardinger Photo/C. K. Marsh, Jr. Collection)

Top Left: Even thought diesel switcher No. 1900 is lettered for the ACL and displays the company's herald, you won't find it listed on the railroad's roster of motive power. In 1939, the ACL was in the market for a diesel locomotive that could replace its steam powered yard engines. It tested an EMC SW-1 and this Alco HH-660 and found both to be inadequately powered to handle the increasing traffic that was being handled through the large terminals. The EMC SW-1 became Richmond Terminal No. 1 (where it briefly switched passengers trains at Richmond's Broad Street Station) and HH-660 No. 1900 was eventually sold by Alco to the Lehigh Valley Railroad.

Bottom Left: The ACL continued to experiment with various types of diesel switchers and in 1941 it placed orders with three separate builders (Alco, Baldwin and EMD) to begin the dieselization of its fleet of yard locomotives. Initially, three Baldwin VO-1000 type switchers were assigned to Rocky Mount, North Carolina, while one EMC NW2 and one Alco S2 were assigned to Florence, South Carolina. Baldwin 1000-horsepower VO-1000 No. 616 was built in 1943 and is seen here in its original ACL paint scheme.

(Both: ACL Photo)

Top Left: The unusual piping shown here on Alco S2 No. 636 is actually a large loop antennae. In October of 1947, the ACL placed into operation its first radio communication system between the yardmaster offices and its yard locomotives at Rocky Mount, North Carolina. Known as the "FM Inductive Train Telephone Communication System", transmissions were accomplished by means of electro-magnetic waves of low frequencies impressed by induction upon adjacent way-side lines wires and the rails. Diesel locomotives such as the 636 carried large loop antennae to send and receive transmissions.

Bottom Left: Alco S2 No. 32 was built in 1944 and originally delivered to the ACL as 1000-horsepower switcher No. 620. It was renumbered in 1955 and, in 1956, it was rebuilt by EMD and repowered with a 12-cylinder engine to change its rating to 1200-horsepower. Like all of the ACL switchers, it was equipped with a modern FM radio system. However, it was not equipped with multiple controls. The switcher is seen here freshly painted in the black and yellow paint scheme after its rebuild by EMD. Note the stepped hood that was required to house the taller EMD 12-cylinder, 567 engine.

(Both: ACL Photo)

The ACL's first Alco-built diesel locomotives were six 1000-horsepower S2 switchers that were delivered in in 1942. No. 612, one of the first six Alco switchers, is shown in its original paint scheme. In June of 1942, three Alco S2 switchers (the 610, 612 and 614) were placed in service at the Wilmington, North Carolina terminal. The ACL originally owned eighteen Alco S2 switchers variously numbered between 602 and 642. They were renumbered as Nos. 26-43 in 1955 and, in 1966, the ACL acquired three former RF&P S2's and added them to its roster as Nos. 44-46.

(ACL Photo)

In January of 1940, the ACL received one NW2 1000-horsepower diesel from the Electro-Motive Corporation. Numbered 601, the unit proved so successful that the ACL added five more EMC NW2's (611, 613, 603, 615 and 605) in 1942. The switchers were subsequently renumbered in the series 600-605. NW2 Nos. 603, shown here after having received a new paint job in the late-1950s, retained that number throughout its tenure with the ACL.

(ACL Photo)

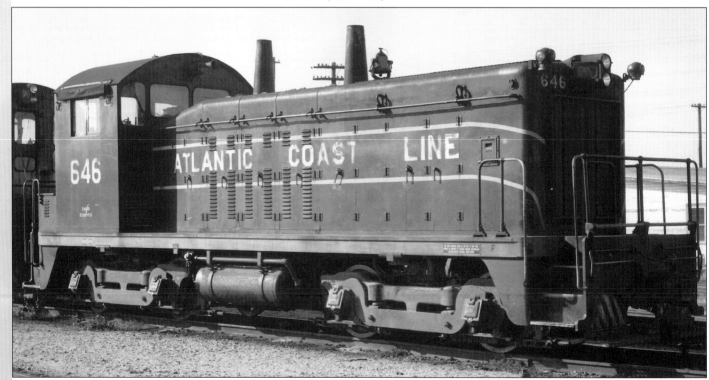

The ACL owned nine EMD SW7 1200-horsepower switchers numbered in the series 643-651. All of these units were delivered to the ACL in April of 1950. When the ACL acquired the Charleston and Western Carolina Railway in 1959, the C&WC's two SW7's (Nos. 800 and 801) joined the ACL roster as Nos. 717 and 718. ACL SW7 No. 646 is shown in service at Lakeland, Florida in the late 1960s.

(Felix Brunot Photo/C. L. Goolsby Collection)

While the majority of the ACL's diesel switchers were 1000 and 1200-horsepower models, the railroad also owned ten 800-horsepower SW8 switchers that were built by EMD in 1952. Numbered in the series 50-59, these switchers were assigned to work at the smaller yards and industries. SW8 No. 57 is at Hope Mills, North Carolina in November of 1963.
(Felix Brunot Photo/C. L. Goolsby Collection)

The largest group of ACL diesel switchers were the sixty-five 1200-horsepower SW9 models (Nos. 652-671) built by EMD between 1951 and 1952. Two additional SW9's were acquired through merger with the C&WC in 1959 and the former C&WC units (Nos. 802 and 803) were assigned new numbers as Nos. 719 and 720 in the ACL series. SW9 No. 682 is shown in its original paint scheme while switching an ACL ventilated boxcar in the early-1950s.
(ACL Photo)

Each FT "A" and "B" unit had 16 cylinder diesel engine-generators of 1350-horsepower and four wheel trucks with a motor on each axle. Initially, the ACL operated its diesel powered freight service with one set of FT "A" and "B" units, such as in this photo of No. 312 and 312-B on a perishable train, each hauling an average of 4,000 tons between Jacksonville, or Waycross, and Florence and 3,500 tons between Florence and Richmond.
(ACL Photo)

Bottom: As originally delivered, FT "A" and "B" units were permanently connected by a ball jointed draw bar and the sections were not to be operated separately. If an "A" unit was out of service for maintenance or repair, the companion "B" unit was rendered inoperable. This situation was finally remedied by the ACL in 1962 when it completed the separation of all its "A" and "B" units. The booster, or "B" units, were equipped with couplers and hostler controls. As seen in this view of booster unit No. 305-B at Rocky Mount on July 9, 1964, the controls were installed on the right front of the unit and a fifth porthole window was added to assist the hostler when moving the locomotive.
(Tom King Photo/C. L. Goolsby Collection)

Top: In 1946, the ACL began to paint the road numbers on the fronts of its FT "A" units because the small nose mounted number boards on the diesels could not be easily observed by the crews of approaching trains. Temporary decals were applied to the engines until such time as they could be worked into the paint shops for this modification. Note the temporary decals on the nose of FT "A" No. 300 as it rounds the curve with a perishable train in 1944.

(ACL Photo)

The addition of painted road numbers were not the only modifications made to the FT's paint scheme. Subsequently, the six inch high lettering was replaced with twelve inch high block lettering and the background of the medallion was changed from aluminum to purple. All of these paint scheme modifications are evident in this photo of FT "A" No. 322 and FT "B" No. 322-B.

(ACL Photo)

Diesel Locomotives **67**

In 1946, the ACL purchased twelve sets of F2 "A" and "B" diesels from the Electro-Motive Division of General Motors Corporation. While the F2's were generally similar in appearance to the FT's, they contained some improvements and features not found on their predecessors. Both the "A" and "B" units were equipped with an improved 16 cylinder diesel engine-generator of 1350-horsepower connected to a 600 volt direct current generator supplying power to the four traction motors. The traction motors were geared to the truck axles with a 59 to 18 ratio making possible a top speed of 80 mph. Belt drives used on the FT's were replaced by individual electric motors driven by an alternator in combination with the main generator. The F2's were also equipped with the latest brake equipment and were approximately four feet longer and heavier than the FT's, producing greater tractive power. This is a side view of F2 "A" unit No. 330 was taken at Jacksonville, Florida.

(ACL Photo)

The F2's were equipped with Clarkson steam generators and had a water capacity of 1200-gallons per unit, which made them available for passenger service. Between Richmond and Jacksonville, F2's were capable of handling seven or eight passenger cars depending on the speed of the train and the number of stops. Each F2 A-B locomotive set could handle between 70 and 80 freight cars. With some of its carbody openings plated over and still displaying shrouded fans, F2 "A" unit No. 335 is at Augusta, Georgia in December of 1964.

(Harold K. Vollrath Collection)

As evidenced by this head-on view of F2 No. 330 on the transfer table at Waycross, the number boards on the F2's, like those on the FT's, made it difficult to discern the numbers of locomotives from the front. Hence, in 1946 the numbers of the F2's were painted on the front of the locomotives and made larger so they were more readily visible to the crews of approaching trains.

(ACL Photo)

Bottom Left: As was the case with the FT's, the F2's were delivered in sets of two 1350-horsepower units. However, the F2 s were coupled by titelock couplers with buffers and diaphragms between the units. Each locomotive was composed of one A power unit which contained the engineer s controls and one "B", or booster power unit. By using titelock couplers in place of the drawbars which joined the FT's, the ACL attained greater flexibility of power in that the sections could be readily separated to form combinations of power to meet varying conditions. The F2 "A " units were numbered 324-335 and the booster units were numbered 324-B to 335-B. F2 "A" unit 330 and "B" unit 330-B are flying the white flags of an extra freight assignment in this photo, but were initially used in both passenger and freight service between Jacksonville, Waycross and Richmond.

(Both: ACL Photo)

In 1948, the ACL purchased twelve F3 A-B locomotive sets from EMD, numbered in the series 336-347 ("A" units) and 336-B to 347-B ("B" units). These F3's had 1500-horsepower and the "A" units were distinguished from the earlier F units by their stainless steel grills and the large nose number boards that did away with the necessity of painting road numbers on the front of the locomotive. The F3 "B" units were the first booster units to have the ACL name rather than the medallion on the side of the carbody. All of the F3's were modified at the Waycross shops in 1951-52 by the installation of D-27-B traction motors. Thereafter, the ACL rated and classified the F3's as F7's.

ACL F3 "B" unit No. 344-B is at Woodland, Georgia on June 13, 1966.

(C. L. Goolsby Collection)

The largest group of cab unit diesels on the ACL were the EMD-built 1500-horsepower F7s. Between 1950 and 1951, the ACL purchased seventy-five F7 "A" units (numbered 348-423) and twelve F7 "B" units (numbered 392-B to 403-B). Six more F7's were acquired in 1959 in the merger with the C&WC. Former C&WC F7 "A" Nos. 900-905 were renumbered as ACL Nos. 424-429. F7 "A" No. 385 and three unidentified booster units are set to depart the yard. Note the Nathan M-5 five-chime horns.

(ACL Photo)

Like the F3's, the ACL F7's had large wrap-around number boards. They also had Mars Headlights, windshield wipers, sun shades, defrosters and train control. This head-on view of F7 "A" No. 349 was taken on the transfer table at Waycross in 1956.

(ACL Photo)

This rear view of F7 "A" No.349 was taken on the transfer table at Waycross after the diesel was painted at the shops in June of 1956. Note the backup light and how the striping wraps around the end of the engine's carbody.
(ACL Photo)

This view looking down on F7 "A" No. 866 provides a detailed look at the Nathan M-5 five-chime horns, rooftop fans, windshield wipers, Mars headlights, large number boards, medallion and pilot's footboards.

(ACL Photo)

The F7's became the standard freight locomotive on the ACL. In this scene, F7 "A" No. 409 and another unidentified F7 "A" bracket an A-B-B-A lashup of FT units on a long freight train a Jacksonville, Florida in the early-1950s.

(ACL Photo)

In 1951-52, the ACL purchased forty-four Passenger-Freight dual-service diesels from EMD. Classified as FP7's, the units were numbered in the series 850-893. These 1500-horsepower "A" units had a gear ratio of 59:18 which allowed them to operate at a top speed of 83 mph. Since they were designed to handle passenger as well as freight service, they were longer than the F7's in order to accommodate a Vapor Heating Corporation boiler. Initially, the FP7's were primarily assigned to local passenger service or to less important trains with smaller consists, such as this passenger train that is being handled by FP7 No. 890 at Bartow, Florida in the early-1950s.

(ACL Photo)

All of the F7's remained in active service on the ACL throughout the 1960s and were on the railroad's motive power roster when the company merged with the Seaboard Air Line Railway in 1967. Most were not retired until 1970-71 when they were traded in by the Seaboard Coast Line Railroad to EMD and GE for new diesels. ACL F7 "A" No. 368 is at Atlanta, Georgia in September of 1961.

(Harold K. Vollrath Collection)

The ACL owned twelve F7 "B" units numbered in the series 392-B to 403-B. F7 "B" unit No. 394-B is at Augusta, Georgia in June of 1962.

(A. M. Langley, Jr. Collection)

As local and secondary passenger service was discontinued by the ACL during the 1960s, the FP7's were found more frequently in freight service. Eventually, nineteen of the units were permanently retired from passenger assignments, their steam boilers were removed and they were reclassified as freight engines. FP7 No. 854, seen here with a northbound freight passing passenger train No. 75 at Selma, North Carolina in February of 1963, retained its boiler and was still on the roster when the ACL merged with the SAL in 1967.

(Curt Tillotson, Jr. Photo)

To begin the replacement of steam locomotives in its passenger service, the ACL purchased two E3-A diesels from the Electro-Motive Corporation in 1939. Numbered 500 and 501, the diesels were delivered in the royal purple and aluminum with yellow/gold trim paint scheme that would become the standard for ACL diesels until 1959. The diesels were purchased for use on the ACL's new streamlined passenger train, the *Champion*, and bore the train's name on their flanks. These diesels were geared for speeds in excess of 100 mph and also operated the *Champion* over the Florida East Coast Railway to Miami and the RF&P Railroad to Washington, D.C. Flanked by steam locomotives and a Pennsylvania Railroad GG1, ACL's E3A No. 501 is at Washington Terminal's Ivy City Engine Terminal in 1939 after having handled the *Champion* over the RF&P.

(Harold K. Vollrath Collection)

Twenty-two slant-nosed E6-A diesels and five E6-B booster units were ordered from Electro-Motive Division of General Motors between 1940 and 1942 as the ACL rapidly converted its passenger motive power fleet to diesel locomotives. The E6As were numbered in the series 502-523 and the booster units were numbered 750-B to 754-B. These units were initially assigned to premier trains such as the *Champion, Vacationer* and *Florida Special* and were used exclusively in passenger service. An unidentified E6A and booster units are shown here passing Moncrief Tower at Jacksonville, Florida with a long passenger train of heavy weight equipment in January of 1947.

(ACL Photo)

The distinctive slanted nose of the E6A's is evident in this company portrait of No. 509. The E6A's contained two 1000-horsepower 2-cycle 12-cylinder V-type diesel engines that were directly connected to 600 volt generators that supplied voltage to operate the traction motors, which in turn were geared to the truck axles with a 52 to 25 gear ratio making possible a top speed of 117 mph. There were two traction motors for each six wheel truck. They had a fuel capacity of 1200 gallons and steam for heating and air conditioning was supplied by a Clarkson steam generator. Other special features included a Mars signal light, automatic train control, cab insulation, windshield wipers, defrosters, titelock couplers and two "Tyfon" horns.

(ACL Photo)

E7A No. 534 and two other "A" units round the curve near Hallandale, Florida on Seaboard Air Line Railway tracks at approximately 80 mph with ACL Train No. 2, the northbound *East Coast Champion* on December 28, 1963. The train was being rerouted over SAL tracks as a result of the strike of the Florida East Coast Railway by its labor unions. E7A No. 534 exhibits the supplementary louvers that were added to the side panels of the E7's by the ACL's mechanical department in the 1950s to afford better ventilation. With the exception of Nos. 524 and 532 that were damaged in wrecks, all of the E7's were still on the ACL's roster when it merged with the SAL in 1967. Most of the units were retired by the SCL in 1971-72.

(E. Verdonok Photo/Jay Williams Collection)

E6A's were operated either singly or in multiple using either two "A" units or an "A" unit and one or more "B" units. The venerable fleet of E3 and E6 units, with the exception of E3A No. 500 that was wrecked and rebuilt as an E8A, was intact on the ACL's motive power roster when it merged with the SAL in 1967. The majority of the units were retired by the SCL in 1970. E6A No. 504, shown in the later black and yellow stripe paint scheme, teams up with two booster units to handle a solid streamlined consist of the *Florida Special* in this ACL publicity photograph.

(ACL Photo)

ATLANTIC
COAST LINE
RAILROAD

"the only **DOUBLE TRACK ROUTE BETWEEN THE EAST AND FLORIDA"**

Between 1945 and 1948, the ACL purchased twenty 2000-horsepower E7A diesel locomotives from EMD numbered in the series 524-543. Ten E7B booster units numbered 755-B to 764-B from EMD were added to the roster in 1945. With the acquisition of the E7's, the ACL could expand the operation of diesel power to all of its New York to Florida passenger trains. In this photo, E7A No. 528 and two booster units roll the northbound *Champion* through Callahan, Florida on August 14, 1949.

(ACL Photo)

The ACL owned ten E7B units. Numbered 755-B to 764-B, they were all built by EMD and delivered in 1945. E7B No. 758-B was photographed in Tampa, Florida by a company photographer in 1950.

(Both: ACL Photo)

The last passenger diesels purchased by the ACL were E8A's. Five were purchased new from EMD in 1950 and eight former Missouri-Kansas-Texas Railroad units were acquired from the Precision National Corporation in 1966. EMD E8A No. 548 is shown with the ACL's only two E8B units, Nos. 765-B and 766-B, in a company publicity photograph. The two booster units were former RF&P booster units 1052 and 1053, and were acquired by the ACL from the RF&P in 1965. The ACL E8's were retired in 1971-72.

The ACL also owned two E8A's that were rebuilt from wrecked E-units. No. 500, shown here in a head-on view, was rebuilt in 1953 from the damaged E3A No. 500, that was wrecked at Fleming, Georgia. E8A No. 532 was rebuilt by EMD during that same year from E7A No. 532 that was wrecked at Dillon, South Carolina.

(ACL Photo)

In 1950-51, the ACL purchased one hundred and fifty-four general purpose combined road and switcher diesel-electric locomotives. Classed the GP-7, and commonly referred to as "Geeps", all were purchased from EMD and were numbered in the series 100-253. They were delivered in the ACL's purple and silver paint scheme, as worn by GP-7 No. 155 in this photo, with the ACL's herald painted on the short hood end. Powered with a 1500 horsepower diesel engine, the GP-7's had two four-wheel trucks and had a continuous tractive effort at 11 mile per hour of 40,000 pounds. With a 62 to 15 gear ratio, they could reach a 65-mile per hour speed and could be operated singly or in multiple, or in a consist with any of the other ACL freight units.

(J. R. Quinn Collection)

Top Right: When operated in through freight service, the GP-7 diesels were operated in multiple with the other ACL freight diesel engines. When operated singly, the GP-7's were found on local, branch line and road switcher assignments. Here, GP-7 No. 234 hustles a southbound local freight through Selma, North Carolina in February of 1963. All of the GP-7's were repainted in the black and yellow paint scheme and were still on the motive power roster at the time of the ACL's merger with the SAL in 1967. Twenty-six additional GP-7's were acquired by the ACL as a result of its merger with the Charleston and Western and the Columbia, Newberry and Laurens railroads.

(Curt Tillotson, Jr. Photo)

Bottom Right: The short hood section of the GP-7's contained space for installation of a 2500-pound steam generator and boilers were installed on a group of the units allowing them to operate in passenger service. A toilet was also located in this section, and the engineer's cab was located just to the rear of the short hood section. Control equipment in the cab was arranged in such a manner that the unit could be operated in either direction. This made them ideal locomotives for operation in outlying yard, local and road switcher service. They were equipped with road-service type 24 RL air brakes. As shown on GP-7 No. 143, the locomotives had dual sealed beam type headlights with one sealed beam unit mounted vertically over the other. If both the front and rear lights were used, the headlight control dimmed the rear light when the front light was bright and vice versa.

(ACL Photo)

The ACL's F units and GP-7's were the mainstay of its freight service motor power fleet until 1963 when the railroad purchased its second group of general purpose diesels. Once again the ACL turned to EMD for its motive power requirements and purchased nine four-axle 2250-horsepower GP-30 diesel locomotives. They were the first new power delivered in the black and yellow stripe paint scheme and were directly assigned to the ACL's premier freight trains on the Richmond-Jacksonville main line. GP-30 No. 905 was photographed shortly after delivery to the ACL in January of 1963.

(ACL Photo)

Diesel Locomotives

Bottom Right: Numbered in the series 900-908, the GP-30's sported a full length rooftop shroud and twin sets of horns that were mounted on both sides of the headlight and numberboard. These characteristic features of the GP-30 are evident in this view of No. 906 and two sister units, shown arriving Woodland, Georgia with a manifest freight in February of 1964.

(C. L. Goolsby Collection)

Late in 1963, the ACL purchased another small group of four-axle diesels from EMD to continue the replacement of its aging fleet of first generation freight diesels. In October and November, EMD delivered six four-axle 2500-horsepower GP-35 diesels numbered in the series 909-914. This company photograph of GP-35 No. 909 was taken when ACL took delivery of the diesel from EMD in October of 1963.

(ACL Photo)

Like the GP-30's before them, the GP-35's were not equipped with dynamic brakes. However, they were the most powerful diesel on the property when delivered and were principally used in the motive power consist of the ACL's important freight trains 109 and 110 that operated between Richmond and Jacksonville. This in-service view of GP-35 No. 912 was taken at Rocky Mount, North Carolina in June of 1964.

(Tom G. King Photo/Robert H. Hanson Collection)

A little over six months prior to its merger with the SAL, the ACL purchased fifteen four-axle 3000-horsepower GP-40 diesels from EMD. Nos. 915-917 arrived in November of 1966, followed closely by Nos. 918-929 in December. The GP-40's were the ACL's first four-axle diesels to be equipped with dynamic brakes and they promptly bumped the GP-30's and GP-35's from the hotshot freight assignments. GP-40 No. 916 is at Manchester, Georgia on December 19, 1966 shortly after entering into service on the ACL.

(C. L. Goolsby Collection)

Almost a third of the ACL's roster of GP-40's help to drag Train No. 105 through Wilson, North Carolina in the Spring of 1967. GP-40 No. 924 and three of its sister units get an assist from an F7A and a GP-7 with their 165-car train of merchandise freight.

(Curt Tillotson, Jr. Photo)

Beginning in 1963, the ACL experimented for the first time with six-axle diesel locomotives. During the final four years of its existence, the railroad would purchase six-axle diesels from EMD, ALCO and General Electric. EMD's first entry in the six-axle arena was the 2500-horsepower SD-35. Delivered in three separate orders between June 1964 and September 1965, the ACL acquired twenty-four of these diesels and numbered them in the series 1000-1023. Nos. 1004 and 1006, shown here at Waycross, Georgia, were delivered in the second order of December of 1964.

(ACL Photo)

SD-35's had the distinction of being the first ACL diesels to be equipped with dynamic brakes. While the SD-35's were used throughout the ACL's system, they were especially effective on the steep grades of the Western Division (former AB&C). SD-35 No. 1002 is shown heading up a Western Division freight train at Manchester, Georgia on August 27, 1964.

(C. L. Goolsby Collection)

In December of 1966, the ACL purchased ten six-axle 3600-horsepower SD-45 diesel engines from EMD. Numbered in the series 1024-1033, they were the most powerful diesels on the ACL and were also geared for high speed service. SD-45 No. 1025 is at Rocky Mount, North Carolina on April 1, 1967.

(Warren L. Calloway Photo)

While the SD-45's were primarily assigned to handle tonnage trains over the more significant grades on the former C&WC and AB&C routes, they were also utilized throughout the ACL system. Here, SD-45 No. 1031 is shown arriving at RF&P's Acca Yard in Richmond, Virginia with northbound Train No. 110 in 1966.

(William E. Griffin, Jr. Photo)

In 1963, the ACL quit its long standing practice of purchasing diesel road service locomotives only from EMD. In December of that year, the railroad acquired its first road service diesels from both General Electric and Alco. They were also the ACL's first six-axle diesels, preceding the arrival of EMD's SD-35's by almost six months. In December of 1963, the ACL was the first railroad to purchase Alco's new Century 628, a 2750-horsepower diesel locomotive, that was hyped by Alco as the most powerful single-engine diesel ever produced in the United States. Manufactured at Alco's Schenectady plant, the ACL purchased eleven of the new diesels and numbered them in the series 2000-2010. C-628 Nos. 2002, 2000 and 2003 head up an ACL freight train in the company photograph of the new diesels.

(ACL Photo)

As was the case with the other new six-axle diesels, the ACL assigned the new C-628's to handle the tonnage freight trains over the grades of its Western Division. C-628 No. 2009 gets an assist from two sister units as its handles its merchandise freight train through Valdosta, Georgia on September 5, 1965.

(Felix Brunot Photo/Robert H. Hanson Collection)

The first General Electric built road service diesels also arrived on the ACL in December of 1963. The ACL first leased and then purchased four GE six-axle 2500-horsepower U25C diesels that were assigned road numbers 3000-3004. Three of these units—the 3001, 3004 and 3000—were posed for this company portrait. The original four U25C were delivered without dynamic brakes, but they were later upgraded with this braking system by the ACL's mechanical department.

(ACL Photo)

The new GE U25C's were so successful that the ACL acquired fourteen additional units of the model, numbering them 3004-3020. These units came equipped with dynamic brakes and they were immediately placed in service on the Western Division. U25C No. 3003 leads two sister units with a long tonnage train at Valdosta, Georgia in the summer of 1964.

(Felix Brunot Photo)

In 1965 and 1966, the ACL continued to purchase new diesel locomotives from GE and Alco. In July of 1965, the ACL purchased its first Century 630 diesel from Alco. Assigned road number 2011 by the ACL, this six-axle diesel had 3000-horsepower and delivered 85,800 pounds of tractive effort at 10.5 mph. Two additional C-630's, numbered 2012 and 2013, were acquired in December of 1965. The 2013 is shown in service at Manchester, Georgia on March 23, 1966.
(C. L. Goolsby Collection)

In 1966, the ACL also purchased GE's new 3000-horsepower model diesel locomotive. In November of that year, the ACL added four six-axle GE U30C's to its motive power roster. Assigned road numbers 3021-3024, they and the EMD SD-45's were the last six-axle diesels built for the ACL prior to its merger with the SAL. U30C No. 3024 is at Manchester, Georgia in December of 1966.
(C. L. Goolsby Collection)

The last diesel locomotives purchased by the ACL prior to its merger with the SAL were four GE U30B's. These four-axle 3000-horsepower diesels were assigned road numbers 975-978 and arrived on the property in February of 1967. U30B No. 977 is at Atlanta, Georgia on August 13, 1967.
(O. W. Kimsey, Jr. Photo/Robert H. Hanson Collection)

PASSENGER SERVICE
EAST COAST SERVICE

Henry M. Flagler, the millionaire associate of John D. Rockefeller in the Standard Oil Company, made his first visit to Florida in 1883. Always the astute businessman, he was immediately impressed with the invisible wealth of the state and its potential for development. Flagler sensed that the state's lack of hotel accommodations and transportation offered enormous business opportunities. He launched his first building venture in Florida with the construction of the lavish Ponce de Leon Hotel at St. Augustine. It would soon be followed by other luxurious Flagler hotels at Ormond, Palm Beach and Miami. As Flagler built hotels along the east coast of Florida, he also built a railroad. Flagler entered the railroad business in 1885 when he purchased the Jacksonville-St. Augustine and Halifax River Railroad, the precursor line of his Florida East Coast Railway. The magnificent Flagler hotels attracted the rich and famous to Florida. Most of the them came by train and, beginning in 1888, they came on board the ACL's *Florida Special*

In 1889, Henry Flagler built the first iron bridge across the St. Johns River at Jacksonville linking his rail line with that of the Plant System. Flagler then began to acquire other railroads down the east coast of Florida, reaching Daytona in 1892 and Palm Beach in 1894. In 1895, his rail lines were consolidated to form the Florida East Coast Railway, and the following year, the line was opened to Miami. In 1895, the operation of the *Florida Special* (its name was shortened from the *New York and Florida Special*), was operating daily except Sunday and was operating south of Jacksonville over Flagler's FEC to St. Augustine. Eventually, the train would be operated from

New York to Miami on a daily basis during the winter season. For many years, the *Florida Special* operated as an all-Pullman train and was assigned the finest locomotives the railroad had to offer. Here, the *Florida Special* rolls behind resplendent P-5-B Pacific No. 1652 in the winter season of 1930.

(ACL Photo)

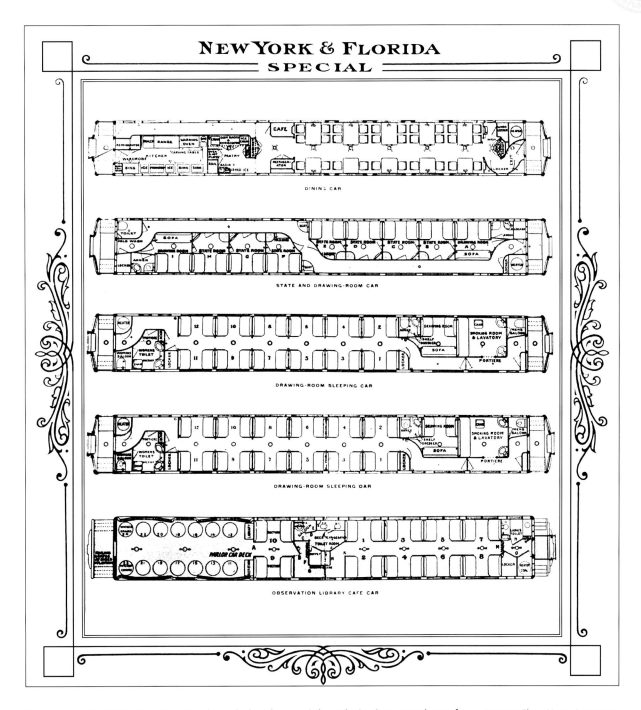

On January 9, 1888, the *New York and Florida Special* made its inaugural run from Jersey City, New Jersey to Jacksonville, Florida. It traveled over the Pennsylvania Railroad to Washington, D.C., thence over the PRR subsidiary, the Washington Southern Railway to Quantico, Virginia, thence over the RF&P Railroad to Richmond, Virginia, thence over the lines of the Atlantic Coast Line System and the Plant System railroads to Jacksonville. The train had only six cars on its maiden trip. There were four sleeping cars, a dining car and a baggage car, with a capacity of 70 passengers. George M. Pullman and a number of Pullman Palace Car Company officials were aboard to place their seal of approval on the equipment they had built for this new service. This diagram from ACL files gives the floor plan of dining, sleeping and observation cars used on the *New York and Florida Special.* Initially, the train operated three times a week on a schedule of 30 hours and 15 minutes. It was the first electrically lighted, steam heated, vestibuled train ever operated in the United States.

(ACL Photo)

The *Florida Special* played an important role in the development of the travel and resort business along the east coast of Florida. By providing a faster, more luxurious and convenient way of reaching Florida, the train was especially instrumental during its early years of operation in bringing in people of wealth to the state. Advertised as the "Aristocrat of Winter Trains", the railroad catered to the high expectations of its discriminating clientele by making improvements each year in both the speed of the service and the luxury of its onboard equipment. Boarding the train in New York for an overnight trip to Florida, these ladies knew that their vacation began the moment they entered the *Florida Special*. The ladies are boarding the train's observation car, which featured a furnished library, ladies lounge and shower bath, and a large smoking room lounge, equipped with a writing desk and the latest periodicals and newspapers.

(ACL Photo)

In addition to its Pullman sleepers, dining car and observation lounge, the *Florida Special* also featured a unique Recreation Car, specially designed to provide facilities for the entertainment of its passengers. The car was under the supervision of an experienced hostess, who directed activities such as contract bridge games. A full-length motion picture was shown every afternoon and after dinner there was dancing to music furnished by a three piece orchestra.

(ACL Photo)

★ THE SCHEDULE ★

Southbound Daily Nos. 133-87	Eastern Standard Time			Northbound Daily Nos. 88-140
1:15 P. M.	Lv. New York (Penna. Sta.)	P. R. R.	Ar.	5:50 P. M.
1:10 P. M.	Lv. New York (Hud. Term.)	P. R. R.	Ar.	d5:55 P. M.
1:13 P. M.	Lv. Jersey City (H. & M. Sta.)	P. R. R.	Ar.	d5:52 P. M.
1:32 P. M.	Lv. Newark (Penna. Sta.)	P. R. R.	Ar.	c5:32 P. M.
2:21 P. M.	Lv. Trenton	P. R. R.	Ar.	c4:44 P. M.
2:49 P. M.	Lv. North Philadelphia	P. R. R.	Ar.	4:16 P. M.
2:59 P. M.	Lv. Phila. Penna. Sta. (30th St.)	P. R. R.	Ar.	4:06 P. M.
a3:30 P. M.	Lv. Wilmington	P. R. R.	Ar.	b3:35 P. M.
4:37 P. M.	Lv. Baltimore			2:27 P. M.
5:25 P. M.	Lv. Washington	R. F. & P.	Ar.	1:15 P. M.
8:15 P. M.	Lv. Richmond	A. C. L.	Ar.	10:30 A. M.
e7:40 A. M.	Ar. Nahunta (Sea Island, Brunswick)	A. C. L.	Lv.	e11:00 P. M.
9:10 A. M.	Ar. Jacksonville	A. C. L.	Lv.	9:50 P. M.
10:10 A. M.	Ar. St. Augustine	F. E. C.	Lv.	8:44 P. M.
g11:02 A. M.	Ar. Ormond	F. E. C.	Lv.	g7:45 P. M.
11:13 A. M.	Ar. Daytona Beach	F. E. C.	Lv.	7:37 P. M.
11:32 A. M.	Ar. New Smyrna	F. E. C.	lv.	7:18 P. M.
1:50 P. M.	Ar. Ft. Pierce	F. E. C.	Lv.	4:54 P. M.
g2:38 P. M.	Ar. Hobe Sound	F. E. C.	Lv.	g4:03 P. M.
3:12 P. M.	Ar. West Palm Beach	F. E. C.	Lv.	3:37 P. M.
g3:52 P. M.	Ar. Boca Raton	F. E. C.	Lv.	g2:59 P. M.
g4:13 P. M.	Ar. Ft. Lauderdale	F. E. C.	Lv.	g2:38 P. M.
g4:24 P. M.	Ar. Hollywood	F. E. C.	Lv	g2:28 P. M.
4:55 P. M.	Ar. Miami			2:05 P. M.

Reference Marks:
a—Stop to receive passengers.
b—Stop to discharge passengers from south of Washington.
c—Stop to discharge passengers from south of Philadelphia.
d—On Sundays arrive Jersey City 5:57 P. M.; Hudson Terminal 6:00 P. M.
e—Stop to let off or take passengers from or for Richmond, Norfolk and beyond.
g—Stop to discharge or receive passengers from or for Jacksonville and north.

The Fastest Train ★ New York to Florida

The *Florida Special* operated over four different railroads—the Pennsylvania, the RF&P, the ACL and, the FEC. After successfully operating diesel power on the new passenger train the *Champion* in 1939, the ACL and FEC dieselized the 1940-41 winter season operation of the *Florida Special*. ACL EMD-built E6 diesels operated through Jacksonville and over the Florida East Coast to Miami. New ACL E-6 No. 516, with an E6-B and another E6-A, are shown at Hollywood, Florida on FEC tracks with the *Florida Special*. The train is flying green flags indicating that additional sections will follow. The *Florida Special* was so popular that frequently three, four or even six sections of the train were required to accommodate the number of passengers traveling between New York and Florida.
(FEC Photo)

Left: The schedule for the *Florida Special* in 1937, the Golden Jubilee Year—or 50th consecutive year—of the train's operation.
(William E. Griffin, Jr. Collection)

A new *West Coast* section of the *Florida Special* (Train Nos. 287-288) was placed in service in December of 1939 handling Pullman sleeping cars between New York and the Central and West Coast of Florida. The train was not operated after the 1941-42 winter season, its operation being suspended during the years of the Second World War. This train returned for the only 1946-47 winter season, as the west coast sleepers were thereafter handled south of Jacksonville by the *Champion*. Here, the all Pullman *West Coast Florida Special* is shown behind a P-5-B Pacific as the train passes through the city streets of St. Petersburg, Florida during the winter season of 1940-41.

(ACL Photo)

The engine crew of P-5-B Pacific No. 1747 wave to the crew of E6-A No. 508 as the diesel speeds by on the adjacent track at Yemassee, South Carolina with Train No. 88, the northbound Florida Special, in the winter season of 1941. When the ACL received its first passenger diesel locomotives they were assigned to the *Champion* rather than the *Florida Special.* Its motive power was provided by R1 Class 4-8-4's and P-5-A and P 5-B Class 4-6-2's until the E6 diesels arrived in the winter of 1940. These diesels were stenciled with the name of the train to which they were assigned, a practice that was discontinued in the mid-1940s.
(Harold K. Vollrath Collection)

By the winter season of 1940-41, the ACL was operating three *Florida Specials.* The *East Coast Florida Special* (Train No. 87-88) was operating with Pullman sleeping cars between New York (and Boston through cars) and Miami. It also offered reserved, deluxe reclining seat coach service between Washington and Miami. The ACL also operated an *East Coast Advance Florida Special* (Train Nos. 187-188) with all-Pullman service and a *West Coast Florida Special* (Train Nos. 287-288) with Pullman sleeping cars between New York (and Boston) and Central and West Coast of Florida, and super deluxe reclining seat coaches from New York. Only the *East Coast Florida Special*, shown here on the FEC Railway at Hobe Sound, Florida, was diesel-powered during that season of operation.
(ACL Photo)

With brand new E6-A diesel No. 511, an E6-B and another E6-A, Train No. 87, the southbound *Florida Special*, is shown arriving at Miami, Florida on January 8, 1941, marking the 32nd anniversary of the train's service to Miami. The city welcomed the one third of a mile long train with ceremonies that included a birthday cake. The *Florida Special* operated for over sixty years with heavy weight passenger equipment. Between New York and Miami, it operated for many years with heavyweight Pullman sleeping cars of the following configurations: cars with 6 compartments and 3 drawing rooms; cars with 10 sections and 2 drawing rooms; and, cars with 8 sections and 5 convertible (single or double) bedrooms. The *Florida Special* finally received streamlined equipment in 1949, with dining cars, 10 roomette-6 double bedroom sleeping cars and 6 double bedroom bar/lounge cars.

(ACL Photo)

Beginning on December 16, 1965, the ACL commenced operation of the first dome car service between the East and Florida on the *Florida Special*. For the 1965-66 winter season, the ACL leased three B&O Railroad 5 roomette, 3-compartment, 1-single bedroom Budd-built dome sleeper cars that had been used on the *Capitol Limited* between Washington and Chicago. Because of clearances of the First Street tunnel under Capitol Hill in Washington, D. C., the dome cars were only operated between Broad Street Station in Richmond, Virginia and Miami. The B&O dome sleeper *Sunlight Dome* is shown on the rear of the *Florida Special* at Richmond's Broad Street Station in December of 1965. Note the ACL herald at the vestibule door.

(Carlton N. McKenney Photo)

Left: During the streamline era, the *Florida Special* continued to provide its discerning passengers with the services, conveniences and activities that they had come to expect from the train. In the special recreation car, fun for every age group included movies, group singing, bridge, canasta, bingo and a horse-racing game. Another added feature, as shown here, was the modeling of the latest fashions in resort wear by the train's lovely hostesses. Other features included dinner by candlelight, dinner reservations for Pullman passengers and complimentary champagne for all dinner guests. The train also offered onboard telephone service and, in 1964, for the first time in railroad history, it offered televisions in its coach, lounge and recreation cars.

(ACL Photo/ William E. Griffin, Jr. Collection)

Perhaps the most notable of the ACL's year around trains was the *Havana Special* (Train Nos. 75 and 76) that commenced operation in 1878—ten years before the *Florida Special*—as the *New York and West Indian Limited*. Originally, the train operated from New York to Cedar Keys, Florida, later, to Tampa and Key West. In the 1920s, it was advertised as the "Fastest Train in the World for the Distance Traveled". Operating over the PRR, RF&P, ACL and FEC, it made the trip from New York's Pennsylvania Station to Key West in 36 hours and 50 minutes. At that time, it operated daily as an all-Pullman train with drawing room and section sleeping cars between New York, Philadelphia, Washington, West Palm Beach, Miami and Key West. In this view, Train No. 76, the northbound *Havana Special*, is shown near Callahan, Florida on March 9, 1926.

(ACL Photo)

HAVANA SPECIAL

Between

New York - Florida
Havana, Cuba

World Famous Lounge Cars,
Sleeping and Dining Cars and Coaches

DAYLIGHT TRIP ACROSS THE FAMOUS OVERSEAS RAILROAD SOUTHBOUND

DAILY SCHEDULES
(Eastern Standard Time)

Southbound Nos. 111-75			Northbound Nos. 76-110
	Lv Boston ....(N.Y.N.H. & H.) Ar	2.25 PM	
3.30 PM	Ar New York (Penn. Sta.)........ Ar	8.45 AM	
8.55 PM	Lv New York (Penn. Sta.).....(P.R.R.) Ar	6.30 AM	
10.00 PM	Lv New York (Hud. Term.)........ Ar	6.34 AM	
9.50 PM	Lv Newark (Market St.)........ Ar	6.07 AM	
10.22 PM	Lv Trenton................ Ar	4.40 AM	
11.16 PM	Lv North Philadelphia........ Ar	4.28 AM	
11.48 PM	Lv West Philadelphia........ Ar	b 3.51 AM	
11.59 PM	Lv Wilmington........... Ar	2.30 AM	
12.34 AM	Lv Baltimore............ Lv	1.30 AM	
2.07 AM	Ar Washington.....(R. F. & P.) Ar	c 1.05 AM	
3.00 AM	Lv Washington.........(A.C.L.) Lv	10.00 PM	
a 3.25 AM	Lv Richmond............ Lv	7.15 PM	
6.25 AM	Ar South Rocky Mount....... Ar	f 5.20 PM	
9.10 AM	Lv Fayetteville........... Lv	3.32 PM	
d11.10 AM	Lv Florence............. Lv	1.27 PM	
1.00 PM	Ar North Charleston........ Lv	g12 40 PM	
2.55 PM	Ar Charleston........... Lv	11.05 AM	
e 3.35 PM	Ar Savannah............ Lv	9.42 AM	
5.17 PM	Ar Jesup.............. Lv	7.50 AM	
6.32 PM	Ar Jacksonville..........(F.E.C.) Ar	7.15 AM	
8.45 PM	Lv Jacksonville........... Lv	6.20 AM	
10.00 PM	Ar St. Augustine.......... Lv	4.56 AM	
10.50 PM	Ar Daytona Beach......... Lv	11.55 PM	
12.05 AM	Ar West Palm Beach........ Lv	10.00 PM	
5.05 AM	Ar Miami............. Ar	5.15 PM	
k 7.00 AM	Lv Miami......(Pan-American Airways) Ar	3.00 PM	
8.00 AM	Ar Havana...........(F.E.C.) Lv	j 3.45 PM	
10.15 AM	Ar Key West.........(P.&O.S.S.) Lv	j 9.45 AM	
11.50 AM	Lv Key West........... Ar	7.20 AM	
h12.20 PM	Ar Havana...........(A.C.L.) Lv	10 06 PM	
h 6.20 PM	Lv Jacksonville (via Ocala)...... Ar	9.30 PM	
9.45 PM	Ar Clearwater........... Ar	7.15 AM	
6.33 AM	Ar St. Petersburg.......(A.C.L.) Lv	a 1.45 AM	
7.15 AM	Lv Jacksonville........... Ar	8.30 PM	
10.25 PM	Ar Orlando............ Lv	6.00 PM	
c 2.40 AM	Ar Sebring............ Lv	6.25 PM	
7.41 AM	Ar Clewiston........... Lv	10 45 PM	
9.50 AM	Ar Fort Myers........... Lv	8 15 PM	
8.20 AM	Ar Tampa.............		
6.15 AM	Ar Sarasota............		
8.40 AM			

a—Sleepers open for occupancy 10.00 p.m. b—Stops to discharge passengers from south of Washington. c—Sleepers may be occupied until 7.30 a.m. d—Stops to discharge passengers from north of Richmond. e—By Bus from North Charleston. g—By Bus to North Charleston. h—Daily except Sunday and Wednesday. j—Daily except Sunday and Thursday. k—Sleeper may be occupied until 8.00 a.m.
See pages 11-12 and Table No. 1 for complete equipment and schedules.

TRAVEL IN SAFETY

Via The Double Track Sea Level Route

The Atlantic Coast Line received the highest award for Employee Safety for 1930, and would have received it for 1931, had it been eligible under the contest rules. Its casualty rate for 1930 was 1.66, which was lowered in 1931 to 1.10 —the two best records ever made by any class 1 railroad.

SUCH SKILL IN EMPLOYEE SAFETY AUGURS WELL FOR PASSENGER SAFETY

ALL FLORIDA— ALL NEW ENGLAND

The Havana Special's early arrival at New York makes it the logical train for travelers bound for New England's famous resorts; connects at Pennsylvania Station with northbound "Hell Gate Express" arriving Boston 2.25 p.m. Evening departure from Pennsylvania Station at 10.00 p.m. provides equally good connections returning South.

ATLANTIC COAST LINE
THE STANDARD RAILROAD OF THE SOUTH

In January of 1912, construction crews completed the overseas extension of the Florida East Coast Railway to Key West, Florida. For the next 23 years, trains of the FEC, and most notably the *Havana Special*, operated over the 128 mile extension that was advertised as the "railroad that went to sea". Other ads boasted that the traveler could go "out of sight of land by Pullman car". One can only imagine the passenger's view from rear platform of the parlor/observation car as the train pulled across the Long Key Viaduct or the seven mile long Pidgeon Key trestle. Upon arrival at Key West, passengers disembarked and directly boarded ferry boats that were operated by the Peninsular and Occidental Steamship Company for the last leg of their trip to Havana, Cuba. The FEC and ACL touted that: "No other train in the world has feature cars as distinctive and luxurious than the lounge cars of the *Havana Special*." This interior view of the lounge car *Camaguey* on the *Havana Special* was taken at Key West on February 28, 1930.

(ACL Photo)

Top Left: The May, 1932 schedule of the *Havana Special*.

(Ray Sturges Collection)

Passenger Service: East Coast

On Labor Day of 1935, a ferocious hurricane (they didn't name them in those days) swept across the Florida Keys devastating everything in its path. Forty miles of the FEC's over-sea extension was destroyed and rather than re-building this very expensive trackage, the line was abandoned and the sold to the federal government. Three years later, the former FEC right-of way was reopened as a portion of U.S. Highway 1. Destruction of the overseas extension brought an end to the Key West operation and thereafter the *Havana Special* terminated its run at Miami. Nor did it remain an all Pullman train. By the 1940s, it was operating on a more leisurely schedule to serve the Carolinas, Georgia and both coasts of Florida. Sleeping cars were operated between New York and Miami, Tampa, Ft. Myers and Wilmington, North Carolina with coach service available for all points. R1 Class 4-8-4 handled the train from 1938 until bumped from the assignment by the E6's. Here, Train No. 75, the southbound *Havana Special,* is shown making a station stop at Charleston, South Carolina on August 2, 1947. E6-A No. 505 and one E6-B are handling the long train of heavy weight equipment.

(George B. Mock, Jr. Photo/David W. Salter Collection)

Train No. 75, the southbound *Havana Special*, rumbles across the single track main line between Raleigh and Goldsboro of the Southern Railway at Selma, North Carolina in February of 1963 behind No. 502 and two sister E6A's. Long gone were the lounge car that served up ice cream sodas and the full-service dining car. Cafe-lounge cars between Richmond and Jacksonville joined the New York to Tampa and Miami sleeping cars and reclining seat coaches in the train's consist of equipment.

(Curt Tillotson, Jr. Photo)

PALMETTO
Pullmans and Reclining-seat Coaches
Daily Between
New York and The Carolinas and Georgia
Diesel Powered South of Richmond

TABLE E — Eastern Time

Southbound Read Down (NYNH&H175 / PRR 129 / RF&P 77 / ACL 77)	Station	Northbound Read Up (NYNH&H174 / PRR 122 / RF&P 78 / ACL 78)
7.30 AM	Lv Boston........NYNH&H Ar	5.45 PM
12.15 PM	Ar New York Penn. Sta. Lv	1.00 PM
1.30 PM	Lv New York Penn. Sta. PRR Ar	11.50 AM
1.45 PM	Lv Newark............ " Ar	11.35 AM
2.33 PM	Lv Trenton........... " Ar	10.46 AM
3.05 PM	Lv North Philadelphia " Ar	10.14 AM
3.19 PM	Lv Philadelphia, 30th St. " Ar	9.52 AM
3.52 PM	Lv Baltimore........ " Ar	9.08 AM
5.00 PM	Ar Washington....... " Lv	8.00 AM
5.40 PM	Lv Washington..... RF&P Lv	7.20 AM
6.25 PM	Ar Richmond........ " Ar	7.00 AM
8.50 PM	Lv Richmond....... ACL Ar	4.20 AM
9.05 PM	Lv Petersburg...... " Ar	4.10 AM
9.45 PM	Lv Petersburg...... " Ar	3.06 AM
11.20 PM	Ar Rocky Mount..... " Ar	1.08 AM
7.00 AM	Lv Norfolk.......... " Ar	10.00 AM
7.30 AM	Lv Portsmouth...... " Lv	9.30 AM
10.30 AM	Ar Rocky Mount..... " Ar	6.30 AM
2.30 AM	Lv Rocky Mount..... " Ar	11.55 PM
3.57 AM	Ar Goldsboro....... " Lv	10.31 PM
7.30 AM	Ar Wilmington...... "	7.20 PM
11.35 PM	Lv Rocky Mount..... " Lv	12.45 AM
12.09 AM	Ar Wilson.......... " Ar	12.07 AM
12.09 AM	Lv Wilson.......... " Lv	12.02 AM
1.40 AM	Ar Dunn............ " Ar	10.55 PM
2.14 AM	Ar Fayetteville.... " Ar	10.30 PM
2.14 AM	Lv Fayetteville.... " Lv	10.25 PM
3.00 AM	Ar Pembroke........ " Lv	9.47 PM
3.31 AM	Ar Dillon.......... " Lv	9.22 PM
	Ar Florence........ " Ar	8.45 PM
4.35 AM	Ar Florence........ " Ar	8.25 PM
4.55 AM	Lv Florence........ " Lv	7.30 PM
5.45 AM	Ar Sumter.......... " Lv	6.19 PM
6.53 AM	Ar Orangeburg...... " Lv	4.25 PM
9.15 AM	Ar Augusta....... GaRR Ar	2.15 PM
12.30 PM	Lv Augusta......... " Lv	9.00 AM
5.45 PM	Ar Atlanta........ ACL Ar	
	Ar Atlanta......... "	8.10 PM
5.00 PM	Lv Florence........ " Lv	7.26 PM
5.34 PM	Ar Lake City....... " Lv	7.00 PM
5.56 PM	Ar Kingstree....... " Lv	6.39 PM
6.14 PM	Ar Lanes........... " Lv	6.25 PM
6.28 PM	Ar St. Stephen..... " Lv	6.01 PM
6.50 PM	Ar Moncks Corner... " Lv	5.30 PM
7.30 PM	Ar Charleston...... " Ar	4.40 PM
8.00 AM	Ar Charleston |City Market " Ar	5.55 PM
6.45 AM	Lv Charleston |City Market " Lv	5.25 PM
7.35 AM	Lv Charleston...... " Lv	5.01 PM
8.12 AM	Ar Ravenel......... " Lv	4.28 PM
8.42 AM	Ar Green Pond...... " Lv	4.10 PM
9.00 AM	Ar Yemassee...... C&WC Ar	3.40 PM
12.15 PM	Lv Yemassee........ " Lv	2.55 PM
1.05 PM	Ar Beaufort........ " Lv	2.45 PM
1.20 PM	Ar Port Royal...... ACL Ar	
9.05 AM	Lv Yemassee....... ACL Ar	4.10 PM
9.22 AM	Ar Ridgeland....... " Lv	3.48 PM
9.40 AM	Ar Hardeeville..... " Lv	3.30 PM
10.30 AM	Ar Savannah........ " Lv	3.00 PM

EQUIPMENT

Type of Car	Car No. Southbound	Car No. Northbound	Between Accommodations
Reclining-Seat Coaches			Washington-Savannah / Between all points
Diners			Washington-Savannah / Washington to New York
Sleepers	R 500	R 500	Washington-Savannah / 8 Sections, 2 Compt., 1 D. R.
	R 501	R 501	Washington-Wilmington / 10 Roomettes, 6 Dble Bedrooms
	A 158	A 158	New York-Savannah / 14 Roomettes, 2 Drawing Rooms
	A 159	A 159	New York-Augusta / 21 Roomettes
	A 160	A 160	New York-Augusta / 8 Sections, 5 Dble Bedrooms
Cafe-Lounge			Rocky Mount to Wilmington / Florence-Augusta

Bottom Left: In addition to the Havana Special, the ACL's other daily year-round Eastern Service trains were the *Palmetto* and the *Everglades*. The *Palmetto Limited* dated back to December of 1909 with daily service between New York, Savannah and Florida, and connecting service to Wilmington and Augusta. By the 1930s, the *Palmetto Limited* (then Train Nos. 82 and 83) had been reassigned to primarily serve the Carolinas and Georgia, with its southern terminal first at Charleston, South Carolina and then at Savannah, Georgia. By 1940, the train was renumbered as Nos. 77 and 78 and following World War II its name was shortened to the *Palmetto*. Steaming up for another southbound trip with the *Palmetto Limited*, P-5-A 4-6-2 No. 1529 is at Acca Engine Terminal in Richmond, Virginia on March 27, 1940. Frequently, the ACL identified its top trains with sheet-metal running board nameplates, such as the one carried by the 1529 in this photo.
(C. W. Witbeck Photo/Bruce R. Meyer Collection)

Schedule and equipment of the *Palmetto* on April 27, 1952.

Bottom Right: On December 1, 1920, the *Everglades Limited* was established as an ACL accommodation train to operate fast daily service between New York and Jacksonville. By the 1940s, the train's name had been shortened to the Everglades and its numbers changed to Nos. 375 and 376. During the 1940s and 1950s, it operated with standard and section heavyweight sleepers, heavyweight coaches and handled considerable mail and express business. Rolling under a stack of white smoke, an ACL Pacific speeds the northbound *Everglades* with a long train of heavyweight cars through Ways, Georgia on March 29, 1930.

(ACL Photo)

By 1942, the ACL was advertising the *Palmetto Limited* as a diesel powered train to the Mid-South. Here, E6-A No. 522 (stenciled the *Palmetto Limited*) and another E6-A are shown at Savannah, Georgia in September of 1944. At that time, the train offered through sleeping cars between New York, Washington, Wilmington, Charleston, Augusta and Savannah. It also featured dining cars, a lounge car and coaches to all points.

(David W. Salter Photo)

Two E6-A's, led by No. 518, bring Train No. 375, the southbound *Everglades*, to a stop at the passenger station in Rocky Mount, North Carolina. The sun was beginning to drop low in the sky on this cold January, 1963 afternoon as photographer Curt Tillotson recorded the arrival of the ACL workhorse with its heavy train of headend traffic. Gone were the sleeping cars and diner. Now the *Everglades* was an all reclining seat coach train between Washington and Jacksonville with sandwich and beverage service only between Washington and Florence.

(Curt Tillotson, Jr. Photo)

Right: The *Everglades* schedule and equipment on April 27, 1952.

EVERGLADES

Pullmans and Reclining-seat Coaches
Daily Between
Washington and Jacksonville
Diesel Powered South of Richmond

Southbound Read Down NYNH&H173 PRR 131 RF & P 375 ACL 375 FEC 7		TABLE F Eastern Time			Northbound Read Up NYNH&H172 PRR 154 RF & P 376 ACL 376 FEC 8
① **10.00 PM**	Lv	Boston	NYNH&H	Ar	
① 7.10 AM	Ar	**Washington**	PRR	Lv	7.10 AM ①
					10.00 PM ①
① 5.30 AM	Lv	**New York** Penn. Sta.	"	Ar	**8.00 PM** ①
① 5.44 AM	Lv	Newark	"	Ar	**7.44 PM** ①
① 7.11 AM	Lv	Philadelphia, 30th St.	"	Ar	**6.22 PM** ①
① 7.38 AM	Lv	Wilmington	"	Ar	**5.46 PM** ①
① 8.39 AM	Lv	Baltimore	"	Ar	**4.44 PM** ①
① 9.20 AM	Ar	**Washington**	"	Ar	**4.00 PM** ①
10.50 AM	Lv	**Washington**	"	Lv	**3.45 PM**
1.15 PM	Ar	**Richmond**	RF&P	Ar	**1.25 PM**
1.30 PM	Lv	**Richmond**	"	Lv	**1.15 PM**
② **2.00 PM**	Lv	Petersburg	ACL	Ar	**12.30 PM**
3.35 PM	Ar	Rocky Mount	"	Ar	10.55 AM
3.40 PM	Lv	Rocky Mount	"	Lv	10.55 AM
4.11 PM	Lv	Wilson	"	Ar	10.17 AM
4.39 PM	Lv	Selma	"	Lv	9.47 AM ②
5.35 PM	Lv	Fayetteville	"	Lv	8.50 AM
㉗ **6.39 PM**	Ar	Dillon	"	Lv	....
7.25 PM	Ar	Florence	"	Lv	7.25 AM
① **4.30 PM**	Lv	Wilmington	"	Ar	11.15 AM ①
① **8.25 PM**	Lv	Florence	"	Ar	6.55 AM ①
① **11.20 PM**	Ar	Columbia	"	Ar	....
① 1.20 AM	Ar	Augusta	"	Lv	2.10 AM ①
① 2.20 AM	Lv	Augusta	"	Lv	1.30 AM ①
① 7.00 AM	Ar	Atlanta	GaRR	Ar	**9.00 PM** ①
7.55 PM	Lv	Florence	ACL	Ar	7.00 AM
8.21 PM	Ar	Lake City	"	Lv	6.20 AM
8.38 PM	Ar	Kingstree	"	Lv	5.55 AM
8.50 PM	Ar	Lanes	"	Lv	5.40 AM
....	Ar	St. Stephen	"	Lv	5.25 AM
....	Ar	Moncks Corner	"	Lv	5.00 AM
9.40 PM	Ar	Charleston	"	Lv	4.27 AM
⑯ **10.10 PM**	Ar	Charleston	"	Lv	3.37 AM ⑯
⑯ **9.00 PM**	Lv	City Market	"	Ar	4.52 AM ⑯
9.50 PM	Lv	Charleston	"	Ar	4.22 AM
10.45 PM	Ar	Yemassee	"	Lv	3.35 AM
12.20 AM	Ar	Savannah	"	Lv	2.30 AM
12.35 AM	Lv	Savannah	"	Ar	2.20 AM
(80) 3.30 AM	Ar	**Jacksonville**	"	Lv	**11.25 PM** (81)
① 4.20 AM	Lv	**Jacksonville**	FEC	Ar	**8.25 PM** ①
① 9.38 AM	Ar	West Palm Beach	"	Lv	**2.41 PM** ①
① 11.20 AM	Ar	**Miami**	"	Lv	**1.00 PM** ①

EQUIPMENT

Type of Car	Car No. South-bound	Car No. North-bound	Between	Accommodations
Reclining-Seat Coaches			Washington-Jacksonville	
			Washington-Florence	
Diner			Between all points	
Sleeper	R 503	R 503	Washington-Florence	
			Washington-Jacksonville	8 Sections, 2 Compt., 1 D. R.

REFERENCE NOTES

① Via connecting train.
② Flag stop to receive or discharge passengers.
③ ACL tickets honored on buses of Service Bus Lines, Inc., between Nahunta and Brunswick, at no additional cost. Baggage, including trunks, may be checked through to and from Brunswick on presentation of through ticket.
⑧ Coach passengers should use PRR Train 126 leaving Washington 8.00 AM.
⑪ Sleeper may be occupied until 7:00 AM.
⑯ Via bus between Charleston and Charleston City Market.
⑰ Train 175 operates Mondays, Wednesdays and Fridays only.
⑱ Train 176 operates Tuesdays, Thursdays and Saturdays only.
⑳ Via bus between ACL Passenger Terminal, Water and Matthews Street, Norfolk, and ACL Portsmouth Station.
㉗ Stops to receive revenue passengers for Florence and stations south and west thereof.
㊶ Mail stop daily except Sunday—also receive or discharge passengers.
(51) Mail stop daily except Sunday—Also receive or disсharge passengers.
(54) Pullman service available for revenue passengers from Fort Myers to Naples daily, except Sunday.
(80) Sleepers may be occupied until 7.30 AM.
(81) Sleepers open for occupancy at 9.30 PM.

MIAMIAN

Pullman-Coach Train • All seats reserved
Daily Between
New York-Washington and Miami
Diesel Powered South of Richmond

Read Down		Read Up
Southbound NYNH&H 3 PRR 133 RF&P 7 ACL 7 FEC 7	**TABLE A** Eastern Time	**Northbound** NYNH&H176 PRR 106 RF&P 8 ACL 8 FEC 8
① 11.30 PM	Lv Boston............NYNH&H Ar	7.25 PM ①
① 5.20 AM	Ar New York Gd. Cen. Ter. " Lv	
	Ar New York Penn. Sta. " Lv	3.00 PM ①
10.25 AM	Lv New York Penn. Sta.... PRR Ar	2.25 PM
10.40 AM	Lv Newark................... Ar	2.10 PM
11.26 AM	Lv Trenton................. Ar	1.25 PM
11.55 AM	Lv North Philadelphia...... Ar	12.55 PM
12.05 PM	Lv Philadelphia, 30th St... " Ar	12.45 PM
12.34 PM	Lv Wilmington............. Ar	12.17 PM
1.40 PM	Lv Baltimore.............. Ar	11.16 AM
2.25 PM	Ar Washington........... Ar	10.35 AM
2.45 PM	Lv Washington.......... Lv	10.10 AM
5.15 PM	Lv Richmond............RF&P Ar	7.40 AM
㉖ 5.44 PM	Lv Petersburg.........ACL Lv	7.05 AM ②
7.08 PM	Lv Rocky Mount......... Ar	5.35 AM
7.36 PM	Lv Wilson............. " Ar	
9.01 PM	Lv Fayetteville....... " Ar	
10.30 PM	Lv Florence........... " Ar	3.45 AM ②
....	Ar Charleston....... " Ar	2.20 AM
....	Ar Charleston City Market... Lv	12.46 AM
....	Ar Folkston........ " Lv	11.56 PM ⑯
4.00 AM	Ar Jacksonville..... " Lv	9.33 PM
4.20 AM	Lv Jacksonville........ Lv	8.55 PM
4.56 AM	Ar St. Augustine....FEC Lv	8.25 PM
5.50 AM	Ar Daytona Beach...... " Lv	7.40 PM
6.10 AM	Ar New Smyrna Beach... " Lv	6.42 PM
7.10 AM	Ar Cocoa-Rockledge... " Lv	6.14 PM
7.30 AM	Ar Melbourne........ " Lv	5.07 PM
8.04 AM	Ar Vero Beach........ " Lv	4.47 PM
8.22 AM	Ar Fort Pierce....... " Lv	4.15 PM
9.38 AM	Ar West Palm Beach... " Lv	3.58 PM
9.51 AM	Ar Lake Worth....... " Lv	2.41 PM
10.05 AM	Ar Delray Beach..... " Lv	2.24 PM
10.38 AM	Ar Fort Lauderdale... " Lv	2.09 PM
10.52 AM	Ar Hollywood....... " Lv	1.37 PM
11.20 AM	Ar Miami........... " Lv	1.00 PM

EQUIPMENT

Special Service Charge in Reserved Seat Coach. See Page 26.

Type of Car	Car No.		Between Accommodations
	South- bound	North- bound	
Coaches	M 20	M 20	New York-Miami 54 Reclining, reserved seats
	M 21	M 21	New York-Miami 54 Reclining, reserved seats
	M 22	M 22	New York-Miami 54 Reclining, reserved seats
	M 23	M 23	New York-Miami 54 Reclining, reserved seats
	M 24	M 24	New York-Miami 54 Reclining, reserved seats
Tavern-Lounge Diner			New York-Miami
Sleepers	A 174	F 174	New York-Miami
	A 175	F 175	New York-Miami 7 Compartments, Bar-Lounge
	A 176	F 176	New York-Miami 8 Sections, 1 D.R., 3 Dble B.R.
	A 177	F 177	New York-Miami 10 Roomettes, 6 Dble Bedrooms
	R 507	R 507	New York-Miami 10 Roomettes, 6 Dble Bedrooms Washington-Miami 10 Roomettes, 6 Dble Bedrooms

REFERENCE NOTES

① Via connecting train.
② Flag stop to receive or discharge passengers.
③ ACL tickets honored on buses of Service Bus Lines, Inc., between Nahunta and Brunswick, at no additional cost.
⑯ Via bus between Charleston and Charleston City Market.
⑯ Via bus between ACL Passenger Terminal, Water and Matthews Street, Norfolk, and ACL Portsmouth Station.
㉕ Stops to discharge or receive passengers from or for Richmond and stations north thereof.
㉖ Stops to receive passengers for Florence and stations south thereof.

On December 1, 1927, the ACL inaugurated the *Miamian* (Train Nos. 71 and 72) as a deluxe all-Pullman winter seasonal train operating between New York and Miami. Promoted as the "Train of Society", it offered "one night out" service with a morning departure from New York's Pennsylvania Station and a 33-hour running time to Miami. In the 1920s, the train departed Jacksonville over the FEC at 9:30 a.m. and arrived in Miami at 6:15 p.m. giving its passengers an all-daylight run through the state of Florida. It featured dining, club and observation cars along with its open section, drawing room and compartment sleeping cars. In this superb action photo, Second 71, the second section of Train No. 71, the southbound *Miamian*, rushes by with a charging P-5-A Pacific and a dozen heavyweight sleepers enroute to Jacksonville Terminal. The action occurred at 9:05 a.m. on the morning of February 10, 1927 just north of Jacksonville, Florida.

(ACL Photo)

The schedule and equipment of the *Miamian* on April 27, 1952.

Top Left: In the later years of its operation, the *Miamian* was renumbered and operated as Train Nos. 7 and 8. The schedule and nature of the train's operation was also frequently adjusted by the ACL. It did not operate during the years of the Second World War, then returned as a seasonal all-Pullman winter train 1946. Coaches were added in 1947 and it operated on a year round basis briefly in the early-1950s. By the 1959-60 winter season, it was again operating as a seasonal train on an every third day schedule and was finally discontinued following the 1961-62 season. The *Miamian* also operated during the 1950s and 1960s with varying consists of heavyweight and lightweight equipment. It had an all-heavyweight consist when Train No. 7 was photographed behind three E7's (led by E7A No. 529) at Callahan, Florida on January 1, 1947.

(ACL Photo)

Bottom Right: While the resorts on the west coast of Florida were no match during the 1920s for those that had been built by Henry Flagler on Florida's east coast, the ACL offered deluxe rail service to both coasts of the Sunshine State. Inaugurated along with the *Miamian* on December 1, 1927 was the *Gulf Coast Limited*, which operated between New York and the Central and West Coast of Florida. Designated as Train Nos. 73 and 74, the *Gulf Coast Limited* operated from Jacksonville to Clearwater, the Belleview-Biltmore Hotel and St. Petersburg via Gainesville and Ocala. The train featured lounge and dining cars, as well as sleeper and coach service from New York to St. Petersburg. The train also featured a parlor-observation car with the train's name on its drumhead, as seen in this view taken at St Petersburg during the first season of the train's operation in 1927.

(ACL Photo)

The equipment and schedule of the *Gulf Coast Limited* in January of 1937.

GULF COAST LIMITED
between
NEW YORK, BOSTON and CENTRAL, SOUTH and WEST COAST FLORIDA RESORTS;
also
BOSTON TO PALM BEACH, MIAMI, and EAST COAST RESORTS

SCHEDULE—DAILY
(Eastern Standard Time)

Southbound Nos. 119-73	Station		Northbound Nos. 74-136
n 8.30 AM	Lv BOSTON	(N.Y.N.H.& H.)	b 8.45 PM
n 9.30 AM	Lv PROVIDENCE	"	b 7.45 PM
n10 46 AM	Lv NEW LONDON	"	b 6.29 PM
10.15 AM	Lv SPRINGFIELD	"	
n11.51 AM	Lv NEW HAVEN	"	
n 5.50 PM	Ar WASHINGTON		7.15 PM
2.05 PM	Lv NEW YORK (Penna. Sta.)	(P.R.R.)	b 5.25 PM
2.00 PM	Lv NEW YORK (Penna. Sta.)	"	b11.30 AM
2.22 PM	Lv NEWARK (Penna. Term.)	"	
3.39 PM	Lv NORTH PHILADELPHIA	"	3 20 PM
3.49 PM	Lv PHILADELPHIA (Penna. Sta., 30th St.)	"	3.21 PM
c 4.21 PM	Lv WILMINGTON	"	3.01 PM
5.30 PM	Lv BALTIMORE	"	1.46 PM
6.40 PM	Lv WASHINGTON	"	1.36 PM
9.25 PM	Lv RICHMOND	(R.F.& P.)	1.05 PM
	Ar ROCKY MOUNT	(A.C.L.)	12.00 N'N
3.06 AM	Ar WILSON	"	10.30 AM
m 4.54 AM	Ar FLORENCE	"	7.40 AM
7.05 AM	Ar CHARLESTON, NORTH STATION	"	g 5.08 AM
e 8.50 AM	Ar SAVANNAH	"	g 4.35 AM
10.30 AM	Ar NAHUNTA (Brunswick, Sea Island)	"	1.39 AM
10.55 AM	Ar JACKSONVILLE	"	11.45 PM
12.35 PM	Lv JACKSONVILLE	"	9.45 PM
1.40 PM	Ar GAINESVILLE	"	e 7.45 PM
4.45 PM	Ar OCALA	"	6.30 PM
j 4.56 PM	Ar CLEARWATER	"	6.05 PM
j 5.35 PM	Ar BELLEVIEW-BILTMORE HOTEL	"	4.05 PM
	Ar ST. PETERSBURG	"	3.05 PM
10.50 AM	Lv JACKSONVILLE	"	12.05 PM
1.00 PM	Ar DELAND	"	J11.53 AM
1.25 PM	Ar SANFORD	"	J11.20 AM
1.58 PM	Ar WINTER PARK	"	6.10 PM
2.10 PM	Ar ORLANDO	"	3.50 PM
3.00 PM	Ar HAINES CITY	"	3.30 PM
3.52 PM	Ar LAKE WALES	"	2.55 PM
4.50 PM	Ar SEBRING	"	2.40 PM
			1.50 PM
3.40 PM	Ar WINTER HAVEN	"	12.55 PM
6.00 PM	Ar PUNTA GORDA	"	12.05 PM
7.00 PM	Ar FORT MYERS	"	
4.35 PM	Ar TAMPA	"	1.05 PM
6.00 PM	Ar BRADENTON	"	10.41 AM
6.25 PM	Ar SARASOTA	"	10.00 AM
11.00 AM	Lv JACKSONVILLE	"	12.25 PM
11.45 AM	Ar ST. AUGUSTINE	"	10.51 AM
12.48 PM	Ar DAYTONA BEACH	(F.E.C.)	10.35 AM
4.47 PM	Ar WEST PALM BEACH	"	
6.30 PM	Ar MIAMI	"	

No. 73—Gulf Coast Limited (Daily)
Lounge Car......New York to St. Petersburg.
Dining Cars......Serve all meals.
Sleepers......
Washington to Tampa—10-Sec., 2-D.R.
New York to St. Petersburg—12-Sec., 1-D.R.
New York to Sarasota—10-Sec., 2-Compt., 1-D.R.
New York to Ft. Myers—10-Sec., 1-Compt., 2-Double Bedrooms.
New York to Sebring—10-Sec., 2-D.R. (Tuesdays, Thursdays and Saturdays from New York.)
Boston to Sarasota—8-Sec., 2-D.R. (Sundays, Mondays, Wednesdays and Fridays from New York.)
Boston to St. Petersburg—8-Sec., 2-D.R.
Boston to Miami—8-Sec., 2-Compt., 1-D.R.
Boston to Miami—6-Compt., 3-D.R.
Coaches......Between all points. Through coaches Boston to Washington; New York to St. Petersburg.

No. 74—Gulf Coast Limited (Daily)
Lounge Car......St. Petersburg to New York.
Dining Cars......Serve all meals.
Sleepers......St. Petersburg to New York—10-Sec., 2-Compt., 1-D.R.
St. Petersburg to Washington—12-Sec., 1-D.R.
Tampa to Washington—10-Sec., 2-D.R.
Sarasota to New York—10-Sec., 2-D.R.
Ft. Myers to New York—10-Sec., 1-Compt., 2-Double Bedrooms. (Mondays, Thursdays and Saturdays from Ft. Myers.)
Sebring to New York—10-Sec., 2-D.R. (Sundays, Tuesdays, Wednesdays and Fridays from Sebring.)
Sarasota to Boston—8-Sec., 2-D.R.
St. Petersburg to Boston—8-Sec., 2-Compt., 1-D.R.
Coaches......Between all points. Through coaches St. Petersburg to New York; Washington to Boston.

110

Top Left: Train No. 74, the northbound *Gulf Coast Limited*, with connection cars for the Seminole at Jacksonville, leaves Inverness, Florida over recently ballasted tracks on February 18, 1928. Motive power is provided by P-4 Class Pacific No. 461 that has its train of heavyweight coaches and sleepers rolling under a clear stack.

Bottom Left: Prior to the establishment of the *Gulf Coast Limited* in 1927, the ACL operated two trains from Jacksonville Terminal to the West Coast of Florida that were key to the development of the resort and tourist business in that part of the state. Those two trains were the *Tampa Special* and the *Pinellas Special* and during Florida boom years of the early-1920s they were pioneer tourist trains to the cities of the Gulf Coast. The *Tampa Special* was inaugurated on November 3, 1913 to operate between Jacksonville and Tampa. The *Pinellas Special* was inaugurated on March 17, 1914 to operated between Jacksonville and St. Petersburg. Both trains departed from Jacksonville Terminal and operated with through Pullman cars from various points in the Northeast and Midwest. Both trains featured observation cars and are shown in this 1925 photo at Jacksonville Terminal.

(Both: ACL Photo)

The southbound *Tampa Special*, Train No. 91, is shown rounding a curve enroute to its namesake city behind P-2 Pacific No. 400 on January 8, 1925. The Tampa Special was equipped with steel coaches and Pullman sleeping, parlor and observation cars. It offered broiler menu service in its dining car and carried through Pullman sleeping cars between Tampa and Washington and between Tampa and Boston, in connection with the *Everglades Limited*. Northbound, in reached Jacksonville in time for all outgoing evening trains, thereby affording a choice of connections to the North and West with the *Dixie Flyer*, the *Seminole Limited*, the *Southland*, the *St. Louis-Jacksonville Express* and the *Everglades Limited*.

(ACL Photo)

Top: An immaculately clean P-3 Class Pacific No. 431, decorated with candlesticks and a sheet-metal nameplate, propels a five-car southbound *Pinellas Special* around a curve at Tarpon Springs, Florida on the line from Trilby to St. Petersburg. Named for the Pinellas Peninsula that separates Tampa Bay from the Gulf of Mexico, the *Pinellas Special* was equipped with steel coaches, Pullman-sleeping, parlor, dining and observation cars. The ACL promotional literature hyped it as: "a complete tourist train, not excelled by any train operated to any resort section of the country". Through Pullman cars were operated on this train between St. Petersburg and Washington, Cleveland, Akron, Grand Rapids and Indianapolis.

Bottom: The *Pinellas Special* is shown at the St. Petersburg, Florida passenger station, the southern terminal for the train. It operated from Jacksonville to St. Petersburg via Gainesville, Ocala, Leesburg and Trilby with stops in Clearwater and the Biltmore Hotel at Belleview. The Biltmore hotel and resort, located just south of Clearwater, had its own spur track off the ACL's main line and the *Pinellas Special* backed across its grounds, allowing the passengers to detrain directly at the hotel.

(Both: ACL Photo)

Passenger Service: East Coast

On December 15, 1938, the ACL inaugurated a new service for the 1938-39 winter season. Named the *Vacationer* (Trains 79 and 70), it was an all reserved-seat, all-coach train operating between Boston and Miami with connecting through car service via Jacksonville to Tampa and St. Petersburg. The coaches, diner and tavern-lounge cars were all of heavyweight construction, the last such equipment to be built by the ACL. The heavyweight coaches were equipped with reclining chair seats, air conditioning, wide picture windows and dressing rooms for men and women. For its second winter season of 1940-41, the *Vacationer* was operated with diesel power over the ACL and FEC and the railroads advertised that the scheduled running time was one and one-half hour faster between New York and Miami than during the previous season. Two of the new ACL E6 diesels are shown here with the all heavyweight coach *Vacationer* on FEC tracks at Stuart, Florida during the 1940-41 winter season.

(ACL Photo)

The marketing goal of the *Vacationer* was to offer the public an inexpensive, yet well-appointed alternative to travel in Pullman sleeping cars between the Northeast and Florida. The train was staffed with a uniformed passenger representative, coach attendants and maid. The tavern-lounge car was radio equipped and the train's two dining cars offered low priced meals. Passengers are shown in one of the *Vacationer's* diners in this photo. The *Vacationer* did not operate during the years of World War II, but was established as an all-coach winter season train on December 12, 1946. Pullmans were operated between Washington and Miami during the 1947-48 season and during the following three seasons it was operated as a Pullman coach train between Boston-Washington and Miami, with lightweight equipment added to its consist. It continued to operate as a winter-season alternative to the *Florida Special* until the 1954-55 winter season when its operation came to an end.

Prior to December of 1939, the ACL's Eastern passenger service was being handled in its traditional manner. The year-round service was being protected by its mainstay trains, the *Havana Special, Everglades* and *Palmetto,* with the *Florida Special,* and *Vacationer* added in the winter tourist seasons. In certain years, the *Miamian* operated as a year-round train, while in other years it operated only in the winter season. The equipment was all heavyweight and the motive power was provided by the ACL's stable of 4-6-2 s and the new R-1 Class 4-8-4's. However, over at the ACL's competition, the Seaboard Air Line Railway was implementing rapid changes. Instead of new steam power, the SAL had purchased new diesel-electric locomotives in 1938 and immediately assigned them to its crack winter train, the *Orange Blossom Special*. Then, in February of 1939, it intro-

duced its diesel-powered, stainless steel streamlined coach train, the *Silver Meteor*. Stung by the public's overwhelming response to the SAL's new service, the ACL moved quickly to get back in the game with its own diesel-powered streamlined train. On December 1, 1939, the *Champion* was inaugurated over the PRR, RF&P, ACL and FEC to provide daily service between New York and Miami. This new train was not named for the railroad's soon-to-be elected president—Champion McDowell Davis—but rather resulted from a contest conducted by the railroad. Shown here on the platform of the Pennsylvania Railroad in New York just prior to the *Champion's* inaugural trip to Miami is Miss Betty Creighton of Pittsburgh, who proposed the prize-winning name for the new train. To her right is Lyman Delano, ACL chairman of the board, Mrs. Delano, and George P. James, the ACL's general passenger agent.

(Both: ACL Photo)

Operating on a daily 25-hour schedule between New York and Miami, the *Champion* consisted of three 7-car trains, two of which were owned by the ACL and one by the FEC. The trains were powered by new Electro-Motive Corporation E3-A diesel-electric locomotives and were comprised of a baggage-dormitory coach, four coaches, a dining car and a tavern-lounge observation car, all of lightweight stainless steel construction. The diesels were painted in a royal purple with aluminum and yellow paint scheme that would become the railroad's standard scheme for its road diesel locomotives for almost twenty years. Under agreements with the RF&P, the diesel power initially ran through over that railroad between Richmond and Washington in charge of RF&P crews. North of Washington, the train operated between Washington and New York with Pennsylvania Railroad electric locomotives. The success of the train was quickly apparent and additional equipment was purchased to expand the *Champion* in December of 1940 to a 14-car daily train. This view of a 14-car *Champion* was taken south of Callahan, Florida in 1945. The train is powered by two brand new E7-A diesels (note that the lead unit does not yet have painted road numbers) and has a combination of streamlined and rebuilt heavy-weight equipment.

(ACL Photo)

Passenger Service: East Coast

In the summer of 1941, the ACL expanded the *Champion's* service by establishing the operation of separate trains to both coasts of Florida and adding heavyweight sleeping cars to the consists of each train. The service was initially renamed the *Tamiani Champions*, the first name being a union of "Tampa "and "Miami". In 1944, the *Tamiani* name was dropped and the *Champions* were referred to as either "East Coast" or "West Coast". Following the war years, the *West Coast Champion* would continue to operate as a coach and Pullman sleeping car train, but the *East Coast Champion* resumed its operation as an all-coach train. Lightweight, streamlined sleeping cars were added to the *West Coast Champion* in 1949. Train No. 2, the northbound *East Coast Champion* speeds through Union Jct., Savannah, Georgia on the afternoon of July 4, 1948. Lead unit No. 522 heads up a two-unit motive power consist of E6 diesels with a 16-car train. For the season 1950-51, the *Champion* was expanded to 17-car daily train.

(David W. Salter Photo)

The schedule and equipment of the both *Champions* on April 27, 1952.

*Left:*The *Champion's* Passenger Representative assists three young ladies as they board the train at the North Charleston, South Carolina station on April 8, 1947. The luxury features provided by the train included reserved seats for each passenger and reclining chairs with individual arm rests and foam-like cushions. The lightweight cars embraced the latest developments of the car builder's skill and were equipped with roller bearings, tite-lock couplers and anti-rattlers. Their interior was decorated with scenes of Florida and had individual lighting for each passenger. Large dressing rooms were provides at opposite ends of each car for both men and women. There were also tavern-lounge, tavern-lounge-observation and dining cars. Muzak musical programs were featured in the coaches, lounges and diners. The train was staffed with maids and chair car attendants. The all-coach *Champion* proved to be so popular with the public that the trains were handled at virtual capacity on almost every trip. In fact, the *East Coast Champion*, not the *Florida Special*, was the ACL's leading moneymaking passenger train.

(ACL Photo)

EAST COAST CHAMPION

Pullman-Coach Train • All seats reserved
Daily Between
New York and Miami
Diesel Powered South of Richmond

Read Down Southbound NYNH&H 175 PRR 105 RF&P 1 ACL-FEC 1		TABLE B Eastern Time	Read Up Northbound NYNH&H 14 PRR 104 RF&P 2 ACL-FEC 2
① 7.30 AM	Lv Boston	NYNH&H Ar	
⑫ 12.15 PM	Ar New York Gd.Cen.Ter	Lv	3.25 PM ①
	Ar New York Penn. Sta	Lv	11.00 AM ①
2.35 PM	Lv New York Penn. Sta	PRR Ar	
2.49 PM	Lv Newark	" Ar	10.15 AM
3.34 PM	Lv Trenton	" Ar	10.01 AM
4.04 PM	Lv North Philadelphia	" Ar	9.14 AM
4.14 PM	Lv Philadelphia, 30th St	" Ar	8.45 AM
4.45 PM	Lv Wilmington	" Ar	8.36 AM
5.45 PM	Lv Baltimore	" Ar	8.03 AM
6.30 PM	Ar Washington	" Ar	7.01 AM
6.50 PM	Lv Washington	" Lv	6.20 AM
9.15 PM	Lv Richmond	RF&P Ar	6.00 AM
11.08 PM	Lv Rocky Mount	ACL Ar	3.30 AM
2.17 AM	Lv Wilson	" Ar	1.27 AM
3.42 AM	Ar Florence	" Ar	12.56 AM ③
⑭ 4.12 AM	Ar Charleston	" Lv	10.15 PM
5.35 AM	Ar Charleston City Market	" Lv	8.42 PM
	Ar Savannah	" Lv	7.52 PM ③
		" Lv	7.05 PM
	Lv Augusta	CofGa Ar	11.55 PM ①
5.40 AM	Ar Savannah	" Lv	8.00 PM ①
	Lv Savannah	ACL Ar	7.00 PM
	Ar Nahunta	" Lv	5.34 PM ③
	Ar Brunswick	Bus Lv	3.15 PM ③
㉙ 7.25 AM	Ar Folkston	ACL Ar	
8.10 AM	Ar Jacksonville	" Lv	4.35 PM
8.30 AM	Lv Jacksonville	FEC Ar	4.15 PM
9.06 AM	Ar St. Augustine	" Lv	3.31 PM
10.00 AM	Ar Daytona Beach	" Lv	2.38 PM
10.19 AM	Ar New Smyrna Beach	" Lv	2.15 PM
11.03 AM	Ar Titusville	" Lv	1.28 PM ③
11.20 AM	Ar Cocoa-Rockledge	" Lv	1.10 PM
11.40 AM	Ar Melbourne	" Lv	12.49 PM ①
12.14 PM	Ar Vero Beach	" Lv	12.18 PM
12.32 PM	Ar Fort Pierce	" Lv	12.03 PM
1.05 PM	Ar Stuart	" Lv	11.33 AM
1.48 PM	Ar West Palm Beach	" Lv	10.52 AM
2.01 PM	Ar Lake Worth	" Lv	10.36 AM
2.15 PM	Ar Delray Beach	" Lv	10.22 AM
2.48 PM	Ar Fort Lauderdale	" Lv	9.50 AM
3.02 PM	Ar Hollywood	" Lv	9.38 AM
3.30 PM	Ar Miami	" Lv	9.15 AM

EQUIPMENT

Special Service Charge in Reserved Seat Coach. See Page 26.

Type of Car	Car No. Southbound	Car No. Northbound	Accommodations Between
Coach	CH 1	CH 1	New York-Miami
Sleepers	A 151	A 151	44 Reclining, reserved seats New York-Miami
	A 152	F 152	10 Roomettes, 6 Dble Bedrooms New York-Miami
	A 153	F 153	10 Roomettes, 6 Dble Bedrooms New York-Miami
	A 154	F 154	10 Roomettes, 6 Dble Bedrooms New York-Miami
Diners			6 Dble Bedrooms, Bar-Lounge New York-Miami
Coaches	CH 2	CH 2	New York-Miami
	CH 3	CH 3	52 Reclining, reserved seats New York-Miami
	CH 4	CH 4	54 Reclining, reserved seats New York-Miami
	CH 5	CH 5	54 Reclining, reserved seats New York-Miami
	CH 6	CH 6	54 Reclining, reserved seats New York-Miami
	CH 7	CH 7	54 Reclining, reserved seats New York-Miami
	CH 8	CH 8	54 Reclining, reserved seats New York-Miami
	CH 9	CH 9	54 Reclining, reserved seats New York-Jacksonville
Tavern-Lounge-Observation			54 Reclining, reserved seats New York-Miami

WEST COAST CHAMPION

Pullman-Coach Train • All seats reserved
Daily Between
New York and Tampa-Sarasota-St. Petersburg
Diesel Powered South of Richmond

Read Down Southbound NYNH&H 177 PRR 195 RF&P 91 ACL 91-191		TABLE C Eastern Time	Read Up Northbound NYNH&H174 PRR 194 RF&P 92 ACL 192-92
① 10.00 AM	Lv Boston	NYNH&H Ar	5.45 PM ①
① 2.20 PM	Ar New York Penn. Sta	Lv	1.00 PM ①
3.40 PM	Lv Penn. Station	PRR Ar	12.30 PM
3.55 PM	Lv Newark	" Ar	12.15 PM
4.40 PM	Lv Trenton	" Ar	11.30 AM
5.09 PM	Lv North Philadelphia	" Ar	11.01 AM
5.19 PM	Lv Philadelphia, 30th St	" Ar	10.51 AM
5.48 PM	Lv Wilmington	" Ar	10.22 AM
6.50 PM	Lv Baltimore	" Ar	9.21 AM
7.30 PM	Ar Washington	" Ar	8.40 AM
7.50 PM	Lv Washington	" Lv	8.15 AM
10.20 PM	Lv Richmond	RF&P Ar	5.45 AM
⑩ 10.49 PM	Lv Petersburg	ACL Ar	
① 7.00 AM	Lv Norfolk	" Ar	
① 7.30 AM	Lv Portsmouth	" Ar	
12.17 AM	Lv Rocky Mount	" Ar	3.35 AM
⑫ 12.46 AM	Lv Wilson	" Ar	
3.25 AM	Lv Florence	" Ar	12.35 AM
4.50 AM	Ar Charleston	" Lv	11.02 PM
5.20 AM	Ar Charleston City Market	" Lv	10.12 PM ⑭
6.40 AM	Ar Savannah	" Lv	9.25 PM
7.38 AM	Ar Jesup	" Lv	
③ 8.03 AM	Ar Nahunta (Sea Island)	" Lv	7.53 PM ③
③ 9.30 AM	Ar Brunswick	Bus Lv	5.15 PM ③
9.15 AM	Ar Jacksonville	ACL Lv	6.55 PM
9.50 AM	Lv Jacksonville	" Ar	
10.53 AM	Ar Palatka	" Ar	6.25 PM
11.31 AM	Ar DeLand	" Ar	5.03 PM
12.20 PM	Ar Sanford	" Ar	4.04 PM
12.43 PM	Ar Winter Park	" Ar	3.43 PM
1.10 PM	Ar Orlando	" Lv	3.07 PM
2.40 PM	Ar Lakeland	" Lv	2.50 PM
3.30 PM	Ar Tampa	" Lv	1.28 PM
5.03 PM	Ar Bradenton	" Lv	12.40 PM ①
5.25 PM	Ar Sarasota	" Lv	10.47 AM
		" Lv	10.30 AM
9.50 AM	Lv Jacksonville	" Ar	
11.50 AM	Ar Gainesville	" Ar	6.30 PM
12.55 PM	Ar Ocala	" Ar	4.18 PM
1.45 PM	Ar Leesburg	" Lv	3.07 PM
4.20 PM	Ar Clearwater	" Lv	2.10 PM
5.05 PM	Ar St. Petersburg	" Lv	11.50 AM
			11.15 AM

EQUIPMENT

Special Service Charge in Reserved Seat Coach. See Page 26.

Type of Car	Car No. Southbound	Car No. Northbound	Accommodations Between
Coaches	CW 36	CW 36	New York-Tampa
	CW 40	CW 40	14 Reclining, reserved seats New York-Tampa
	CW 41	CW 41	46 Reclining, reserved seats New York-St. Petersburg
	CW 43	CW 43	54 Reclining, reserved seats New York-Tampa
	CW 44	CW 44	54 Reclining, reserved seats New York-Tampa
	CW 45	CW 45	54 Reclining, reserved seats New York-Tampa-Sarasota
Tavern-Lounge			54 Reclining, reserved seats New York-Tampa
Diner			New York-Tampa
Sleepers	A 166	A 166	New York-Tampa
	A 167	A 167	6 Dble Bedrooms, Bar-Lounge New York-Tampa
	A 168	A 168	10 Roomettes, 6 Dble Bedrooms New York-Tampa
	A 169	A 169	10 Roomettes, 6 Dble Bedrooms New York-Tampa-Sarasota
Diner			10 Roomettes, 6 Dble Bedrooms Jacksonville-St. Petersburg
Sleeper	A 170	A 170	New York-St. Petersburg 10 Roomettes, 6 Dble Bedrooms

Top Left: An A-B-A consist of E-units, with E6-A No. 523 in the lead, roll Train No. 2, the *East Coast Champion*, north of Okeechobee, Florida (on SAL tracks) on a sparkling clear day in December of 1966. ACL passenger trains to and from Miami were being rerouted over the SAL south of Auburndale, Florida during this period account the strike on the FEC. The E6's had over 25 years of service behind them when this photo was taken, but they could still handle their passenger assignments with the speed and dependability required by the most demanding schedule.

(David W. Salter Photo)

Bottom Left: In 1944, the *Coast Line Florida Mail's* name was shortened to the *Florida Mail*. By this time it had become an all-coach train and, three years later, it was reduced to a Richmond and Florence operation. A separate *Florida Mail* train, also operating as Train Nos. 80 and 89, ran between Jacksonville and Tampa. The southbound *Florida Mail* (Train No. 89) was photographed at Winter Park, Florida in July of 1949. The operation of the *Florida Mail* train was discontinued in 1958 and the express and mail business was thereafter handled on other ACL passenger trains.

(Mac B. Connery Photo)

The *Coast Line Florida Mail* (Trains 80 and 89) began operating in the late-1890 s as through local passenger trains between Washington, D. C. and Tampa, Florida. In addition to handling the important express and mail business, they were daily all-stops locals. Primarily all-coach trains, they were unusual locals in that they did offer Pullman sleeper car service during the 1930s. Since the trains consist did not include a dining car, stops for food were made at Rocky Mount and Florence. Train No. 80, the northbound *Coast Line Florida Mail,* is shown crossing the Tar River bridge, just north of Rocky Mount, with double-head P-5-A Pacifics Nos. 1546 and 1538.

(J. I. Kelly Photo/Evan Siler Collection)

ATLANTIC
COAST LINE
RAILROAD

The ACL's Eastern service also included many connection trains that supplied passengers to main line trains of the ACL and other railroads. One such service operated over the ACL tracks between Broad Street Station in Richmond, Virginia and Petersburg, Virginia, where connection was made with the main line trains of the Norfolk and Western Railway. In the late-1930s, there were six pairs of connecting trains operating over the 27 miles

between Petersburg and Richmond. Southbound Local Train No. 25 is shown departing Broad Street Station in Richmond for its afternoon run to Petersburg behind ACL P-3 Class 4-6-2 No. 415 on the first day of January, 1937.
(George E. Votava Photo/Frank E. Ardrey, Jr. Collection)

Another important connecting service was provided on the ACL line between Rocky Mount, North Carolina and Portsmouth, Virginia. For many years, the route was serviced by two sets of trains, one that operated at night (43-44) and another that operated during daylight hours (48-49). Under the atrics of smoke and steam on a frigid winter day, P-5-B Class 4-6 2 No. 1668 gets underway with Train No. 49 on its late morning departure from Portsmouth.
(L. D. Moore Photo)

ACL Norfolk to Rocky Mount passenger train No. 35 is shown at Portsmouth, Virginia as the train prepares to depart for its last run on the evening of May 15, 1954. The train departed Portsmouth at 7:30 p.m. and made its usual leisurely three and one-half hour run to Rocky Mount. For its last run, Train No. 35 was pulled by boiler-equipped GP-7 No. 176. This photograph was taken by Mallory Hope Ferrell, who was working for the newspaper at the time. His photographs and the story of the trains' discontinuance appeared in the April 21, 1954 edition of the *Norfolk Virginian-Pilot*.

(Mallory Hope Ferrell Photo)

The head brakeman is riding the pilot of Class P-3s Pacific No. 449 to flag crossings as ACL Train No. 50 departs Augusta, Georgia in the late 1930s. Trains 50-51 operated from Augusta to Florence, South Carolina, where connection was made with the ACL's *Palmetto*. At Augusta, these trains connected with Georgia Railroad trains for Atlanta, thus allowing the ACL a route for passengers between the Northeast and Atlanta.

(Truman Blasingame Photo/David W. Salter Collection)

PASSENGER SERVICE
WEST COAST SERVICE

In addition to its lucrative Eastern passenger service ferrying travelers between the Northeast and Florida, a number of year-round and winter season passenger trains also operated over the ACL's tracks between the Midwest and Florida. In both its Eastern and Western service, the ACL essentially served as a bridge route since the majority of the trains originated and terminated on connecting railroads. However, while all of the Eastern service was routed PRR/RF&P/ACL/FEC, the ACL trains between the Midwest and Florida operated via several different routes and railroads. This resulted in a variety of connecting service and through car arrangements as well as solid train movements.

The most famous route was the *Dixie Route* which included the Chicago & Eastern Illinois (Chicago to Evansville, Indiana), Louisville & Nashville (Evansville to Nashville), Nashville, Chattanooga and St. Louis (Nashville to Atlanta), Central of Georgia (Atlanta to Albany, Georgia via Macon) and ACL (Albany to Jacksonville).

Top Left: The schedule and equipment of the *Dixie Flyer* on April 27, 1952.
Bottom Left: The first service between the Midwest and Florida to operate over the ACL was the *Dixie Limited*, shown here northbound at Moncrief, Florida on March 9, 1926. Inaugurated on January 5, 1903 between Chicago and Florida, the *Dixie Limited* was initially named the *Chicago and Florida Limited* and was the first deluxe through all-Pullman train to operate between the West and Florida. The *Dixie Limited* offered a popular midday departure from Chicago but required to a two night trip to reach Miami. It operated via the "Dixie Route", as did its companion train, the *Dixie Flyer*. The *Dixie Flyer* provided a night departure from Chicago to Florida and was also inaugurated as an all-Pullman on December 13, 1903. By the 1930s, both trains were operating on daily schedules with deluxe Pullman sleeping car, coach and dining car service. After the Second World War, the *Dixie Limited* ran in combination with the Cincinnati to Florida *Flamingo* until it was discontinued in 1951. After the ACL's acquisition of the AB&C Railroad in 1946, the *Dixie Flyer* was rerouted south of Atlanta over the AB&C line from Atlanta to Waycross.

(ACL Photo)

DIXIE FLYER
TABLE K

Southbound Read down			Northbound Read up
		Central Time	
10.55 PM	Lv Chicago	..............C&EI Ar	
Ⓧ 10.30 PM	Lv St. Louis	..............C&EI Ar	5.30 AM Ⓧ
5.40 AM	Lv Evansville	..............L&N Ar	5.00 AM Ⓧ
10.25 AM	Lv Nashville	............" Ar	10.15 PM
		......NC&StL Ar	5.20 PM
		Eastern Time	
3.55 PM	Lv Chattanooga	.... " Ar	1.40 PM
7.25 PM	Ar Atlanta	.... " Lv	9.50 AM
9.05 PM	Lv Atlanta	.... " Lv	8.00 AM
11.45 PM	Lv Macon	......CofGa Ar	4.53 AM
2.35 AM	Ar Albany	.... " Ar	2.10 AM
2.50 AM	Lv Albany	.... " Lv	2.00 AM
3.50 AM	Ar Tifton	......ACL Ar	12.45 AM
3.50 AM	Lv Tifton	.... " Lv	12.45 AM
5.40 AM	Ar Waycross (Plant Ave.)	" Ar	11.00 PM
6.00 AM	Lv Waycross (Plant Ave.)	" Lv	10.45 PM
7.45 AM	Ar Jacksonville	.... " Lv	9.00 PM
① 9.50 AM	Lv Jacksonville	.... " Ar	6.25 PM ①
① 10.53 AM	Ar Palatka	.... " Lv	5.03 PM ①
① 11.51 AM	Ar DeLand	.... " Lv	4.04 PM ①
① 12.20 PM	Ar Sanford	.... " Lv	3.43 PM ①
① 12.43 PM	Ar Winter Park	.... " Lv	3.07 PM ①
① 1.10 PM	Ar Orlando	.... " Lv	2.50 PM ①
① 1.56 PM	Ar Haines City	.... " Lv	1.56 PM ①
① 2.40 PM	Ar Lakeland	.... " Lv	1.28 PM ①
① 2.52 PM	Ar Plant City	.... " Lv	1.04 PM ①
① 3.30 PM	Ar Tampa	.... " Lv	12.40 PM ①
① 3.55 PM	Lv Tampa	.... " Lv	12.10 PM ①
① 5.03 PM	Ar Bradenton	.... " Ar	10.47 AM ①
① 5.25 PM	Ar Sarasota	.... " Lv	10.30 AM ①
① 9.50 AM	Lv Jacksonville	.... " Ar	6.30 PM ①
① 11.50 AM	Ar Gainesville	.... " Lv	4.18 PM ①
① 12.55 PM	Ar Ocala	.... " Lv	3.07 PM ①
① 1.45 PM	Ar Leesburg	.... " Lv	2.10 PM ①
① 4.20 PM	Ar Clearwater	.... " Lv	11.50 AM ①
① 5.05 PM	Ar St. Petersburg	.... " Lv	11.15 AM ①
① 8.30 AM	Lv Jacksonville	.... "	
① 9.06 AM	Ar St. Augustine	......FEC Ar	8.25 PM ①
① 10.00 AM	Ar Daytona Beach	.... " Lv	7.40 PM ①
① 1.48 PM	Ar West Palm Beach	.... " Lv	6.42 PM ①
① 2.48 PM	Ar Ft. Lauderdale	.... " Lv	2.41 PM ①
① 3.02 PM	Ar Hollywood	.... " Lv	1.37 PM ①
① 3.30 PM	Ar Miami	.... " Lv	1.23 PM ①
			1.00 PM ①

EQUIPMENT

Type of Car	Car No.		Between
	Southbound	Northbound	Accommodations
Coaches			Chicago-Jacksonville Reclining Seats
			St. Louis-Evansville Reclining seats
Diner			Between all points Evansville-Atlanta
Sleepers	51	51	Chicago-Jacksonville 10 Sections, 2 Compts., 1 D. R.
	950	950	Atlanta-Jacksonville 10 Sections, 2 Compts., 1 D. R.
	57	67	Chicago-Evansville 8 Sections, 1 Compt., 1 D. R.
	55	68	Chicago-Evansville 8 Single Bedrooms, Lounge

REFERENCE NOTES
Ⓧ Operates via Perry, Fla.
① Via Tamiami Trail Tours bus south of Tampa.
Ⓧ Coach passengers may also use through St. Louis-Nashville coach leaving St. Louis 9.20 PM arriving Nashville 7.35 AM.

On January 2, 1936, a new service was created between Chicago and Florida with the inauguration of the Dixieland. With a morning departure from Chicago, the *Dixieland* traveled the "Dixie Route" until it reached Atlanta, where it was then routed over the AB&C via Manchester and Fitzgerald, Georgia to Waycross, thence handled by the ACL to Jacksonville. This shorter route via the AB&C enabled the *Dixieland* to become the first through train ever operated on a one-night-out schedule between Chicago and Miami. A similar routing was taken by the *Dixie Flagler*, inaugurated on December 17, 1940 to operate an every-third-day all-reserved seat stainless steel streamlined coach train on a one night out schedule. The *Dixie Flagler* was also equipped with dining and tavern-lounge-observation cars. Belching smoke and rolling at an estimated speed of 50 mph, ACL Class AM-1 4-8-2 No. 7372 passes the yard limit board for Bellwood Yard as it nears Atlanta, Georgia with the northbound *Dixie Flagler*. The former AB&C had used a streamlined Pacific steam locomotive to handle the *Dixie Flagler,* but this locomotive was destroyed in an accident in 1945. The ACL 7372 is in familiar territory. It was a former AB&C and FEC locomotive.

(David W. Salter Photo)

Another route via Albany included the Illinois Central (Chicago to Birmingham), CofG (Birmingham to Albany via Columbus, Georgia) and ACL (Albany to Jacksonville). A route via Montgomery involved the Pennsylvania (Chicago to Louisville via Indianapolis), L&N (Louisville to Montgomery via Birmingham) and ACL (Montgomery to Jacksonville via Waycross, Dothan, Alabama and Thomasville, Georgia). While certain of these Midwestern trains terminated at Jacksonville, others continued on via the FEC to Miami or over the ACL to the west coast of Florida. A fourth route, used only by the Southland, included the Pennsylvania (Chicago to Louisville), L&N (Cincinnati to Atlanta via Knoxville), CofG (Atlanta to Albany) and ACL (Albany to Tampa via the Perry Cut-Off).

These interline passenger operations enabled the ACL to advertise that it offered the largest fleet of trains between the West and Florida. However, since the trains were run over the ACL's rails for relatively short distances, its division of the revenues did little for the bottom line. In a representative year— 1954—about 75 percent of the ACL's total passenger revenues were brought in by through trains running between the East and Florida. About 14 percent were brought in from locals and extra trains and the rest—only 11 percent—came from the trains connecting the Midwest with Florida. Only one of these Chicago to Florida trains—the *South Wind*—survived into the Amtrak era.

DIXIE FLAGLER

Southbound from Chicago via C&EIRR:
April 27, 30. May 3, 6, 9, 12, 15, 18, 21, 24, 27, 30. June 2, 5, 8, 11, 14, 17, 20, 23, 26, 29. July 2, 5, 8, 11, 14, 17, 20, 23, 26, 29 and every 3rd day thereafter.

Northbound from Miami via FEC Ry:
April 28. May 1, 4, 7, 10, 13, 16, 19, 22, 25, 28, 31. June 3, 6, 9, 12, 15, 18, 21, 24, 27, 30. July 3, 6, 9, 12, 15, 18, 21, 24, 27, 30 and every 3rd day thereafter.

Southbound Read down		TABLE G			Northbound Read up
		Central Time			
9.10 AM	Lv	Chicago	C&EI	Ar	5.35 PM
9.24 AM	Lv	Englewood		Ar	5.20 PM
12.35 PM	Ar	Terre Haute		Ar	2.10 PM
① 8.30 AM	Lv	St. Louis	L&N	Ar	
2.50 PM	Ar	Evansville		Ar	
6.00 PM	Lv	Nashville	NC&StL	Ar	11.55 AM
		Eastern Time			8.45 AM
10.15 PM	Lv	Chattanooga		Ar	
1.20 AM	Ar	Atlanta		Lv	6.30 AM
1.30 AM	Lv	Atlanta	ACL	Lv	3.25 AM
7.55 AM	Ar	Waycross (Plant Ave.)		Lv	3.15 AM
8.00 AM	Lv	Waycross (Plant Ave.)	"	Lv	8.45 PM
9.25 AM	Ar	Jacksonville	"	Lv	8.40 PM
9.45 AM	Lv	Jacksonville	FEC	Lv	7.20 PM
10.21 AM	Ar	St. Augustine	"	Lv	7.00 PM
11.15 AM	Ar	Daytona Beach	"	Lv	6.16 PM
11.35 AM	Ar	New Smyrna Beach	"	Lv	5.23 PM
12.35 PM	Ar	Cocoa-Rockledge	"	Lv	5.00 PM
12.55 PM	Ar	Melbourne	"	Lv	3.56 PM
1.28 PM	Ar	Vero Beach	"	Lv	3.35 PM
1.47 PM	Ar	Fort Pierce	"	Lv	3.04 PM
2.20 PM	Ar	Stuart	"	Lv	2.49 PM
3.04 PM	Ar	West Palm Beach	"	Lv	2.19 PM
3.17 PM	Ar	Lake Worth	"	Lv	1.38 PM
3.31 PM	Ar	Delray Beach	"	Lv	1.22 PM
3.42 PM	Ar	Boca Raton	"	Lv	12.57 PM
4.05 PM	Ar	Ft. Lauderdale	"	Lv	12.36 PM
4.18 PM	Ar	Hollywood	"	Lv	12.24 PM
4.45 PM	Ar	Miami	"	Lv	12.01 PM
① 9.50 AM	Lv	Jacksonville	ACL	Ar	6.25 PM ①
① 1.10 PM	Ar	Orlando	"	Lv	2.50 PM ①
① 2.40 PM	Ar	Lakeland	"	Lv	1.28 PM ①
① 3.30 PM	Ar	Tampa	"	Lv	1.03 PM ①
① 5.03 PM	Ar	Bradenton	"	Lv	10.47 AM ①
① 5.25 PM	Ar	Sarasota	"	Lv	10.30 AM ①
① 9.50 AM	Lv	Jacksonville		Ar	6.30 PM ①
① 11.50 AM	Ar	Gainesville	"	Ar	
① 12.55 PM	Ar	Ocala	"	Lv	4.18 PM ①
① 1.45 PM	Ar	Leesburg	"	Lv	3.07 PM ①
① 4.20 PM	Ar	Clearwater	"	Lv	2.10 PM ①
① 5.05 PM	Ar	St. Petersburg	"	Lv	11.50 AM ①
					11.15 AM ①

EQUIPMENT

Special Service Charge in Reserved Seat Coach. See Page 26.

Type of Car	Car No. South-bound	Car No. North-bound	Between Accommodations
Coach	DF 1	DF 1	Chicago-Miami 18 Reclining, reserved seats
Sleepers	DF 92	DF 92	Chicago-Miami 6 Sections, 6 Dble Bedrooms
	DF 91	DF 91	Chicago-Miami 10 Roomettes, 6 Dble Bedrooms
	DF 90	DF 90	Chicago-Miami 5 Dble Bedrooms, Bar-Lounge
Diner Sleeper	DF 95	DF 95	Chicago-Miami Chicago-Jacksonville 10 Roomettes, 6 Dble Bdrms.
Coffee Shop-Lounge Coaches	DF 6	DF 6	Chicago-Jacksonville Chicago-Jacksonville
	DF 4	DF 4	Chicago-Miami 52 Reclining, reserved seats
	DF 3	DF 3	Chicago-Miami 52 Reclining, reserved seats
	DF 2	DF 2	Chicago-Miami 52 Reclining, reserved seats
Tavern-Lounge-Obs.			Chicago-Miami 52 Reclining, reserved seats

Reference Notes: ① Via connecting train.

ATLANTIC
COAST LINE
RAILROAD

The schedule and equipment of the *Dixie Flagler* on April 27, 1952.

CITY OF MIAMI

Southbound from Chicago via ICRR:
April 28. May 1, 4, 7, 10, 13, 16, 19, 22, 25, 28, 31. June 3,
6, 9, 12, 15, 18, 21, 24, 27, 30. July 3, 6, 9, 12, 15, 18, 21, 24,
27, 30 and every 3rd day thereafter.

Northbound from Miami via FEC Ry:
April 29. May 2, 5, 8, 11, 14, 17, 20, 23, 26, 29. June 1, 4,
7, 10, 13, 16, 19, 22, 25, 28. July 1, 4, 7, 10, 13, 16, 19, 22, 25
28, 31 and every 3rd day thereafter.

Southbound Read down		TABLE H	Northbound Read up
		Central Time	
8.10 AM	Lv	Chicago......... IllCen Ar	10.55 PM
8.21 AM	Lv	63rd Street........ " Ar	10.42 PM
9.22 AM	Lv	St. Louis.......... Ar	8.45 PM
1.02 PM	Lv	Carbondale........ Ar	
2.13 PM	Lv	North Cairo....... Ar	5.50 PM
9.50 PM	Lv	Birmingham..... CofGa Ar	4.40 PM
		Eastern Time	9.20 AM
2.20 AM	Lv	Columbus........	
4.25 AM	Ar	Albany.......... " Ar	6.45 AM
4.35 AM	Lv	Albany.......... " Lv	4.45 AM
5.27 AM	Ar	Tifton.......... ACL Ar	4.40 AM
6.50 AM	Ar	Waycross (Plant Ave.).. " Lv	3.38 AM
6.55 AM	Lv	Waycross (Plant Ave.).. " Lv	2.18 AM
8.15 AM	Ar	Jacksonville...... " Ar	2.15 AM
8.40 AM	Lv	Jacksonville...... " Lv	1.00 AM
9.16 AM	Ar	St. Augustine..... FEC Ar	12.40 AM
10.10 AM	Ar	Daytona Beach.... " Lv	11.58 PM
10.32 AM	Ar	New Smyrna Beach. " Lv	11.03 PM
11.30 AM	Ar	Cocoa-Rockledge.. " Lv	10.40 PM
11.50 AM	Ar	Melbourne....... " Lv	9.34 PM
12.24 PM	Ar	Vero Beach....... " Lv	9.14 PM
12.42 PM	Ar	Fort Pierce...... " Lv	8.43 PM
1.15 PM	Ar	Stuart.......... " Lv	8.28 PM
1.58 PM	Ar	West Palm Beach.. " Lv	7.57 PM
2.11 PM	Ar	Lake Worth....... " Lv	7.14 PM
2.25 PM	Ar	Delray Beach..... " Lv	6.58 PM
2.36 PM	Ar	Boca Raton....... " Lv	6.44 PM
2.58 PM	Ar	Ft. Lauderdale.... " Lv	6.34 PM
3.12 PM	Ar	Hollywood....... " Lv	6.14 PM
3.40 PM	Ar	Miami.......... " Lv	6.03 PM
① 9.50 AM	Lv	Jacksonville......	5.40 PM
① 1.10 PM	Ar	Orlando......... ACL Ar	6.25 PM ①
① 2.40 PM	Ar	Lakeland........ " Lv	2.50 PM ①
① 3.30 PM	Ar	Tampa.......... " Lv	1.28 PM ①
① 5.03 PM	Ar	Bradenton....... " Lv	12.40 PM ①
① 5.25 PM	Ar	Sarasota........ " Lv	10.47 AM ①
① 9.50 AM	Lv	Jacksonville......	10.30 AM ①
① 11.50 AM	Ar	Gainesville...... Ar	6.30 PM ①
① 12.55 PM	Ar	Ocala.......... " Lv	4.18 PM ①
① 1.45 PM	Ar	Leesburg........ " Lv	3.07 PM ①
① 4.20 PM	Ar	Clearwater...... " Lv	2.10 PM ①
① 5.05 PM	Ar	St. Petersburg.... " Lv	11.50 AM ①
			11.15 AM ①

EQUIPMENT
Special Service Charge in Reserved Seat Coach. See Page 26.

Type of Car	Car No.		Between Accommodations
	South-bound	North-bound	
Sleepers	CM 31	CM 31	Chicago-Miami 6 Sec., 6 Rmts., 4 Dble Bdrms.
	CM 32	CM 32	Chicago-Miami 10 Roomettes, 6 Dble Bedrooms
	CM 33	CM 33	Chicago-Miami 3 Dble Bdrms, 1 Compt., 1 Drawing Rm., Lounge
	CM 34	CM 34	Chicago-Jacksonville 6 Sec., 6 Roomettes, 4 Dble Bedrooms
Coach	CM 1	CM 1	Chicago-Jacksonville 56 Reclining, reserved seats
Diner			Chicago-Miami
Coaches	CM 2	CM 2	Chicago-Miami 68 Reclining, reserved seats
	CM 3	CM 3	Chicago-Miami 52 Reclining, reserved seats
	CM 4	CM 4	Chicago-Miami 54 Reclining, reserved seats
	CM 5	CM 5	Chicago-Miami 56 Reclining, reserved seats
	CM 6	CM 6	St. Louis-Miami 56 Reclining, reserved seats
Tavern-Lounge-Obs.			Chicago-Miami

Reference Notes: ① Via connecting train.

② Stops to discharge or receive passengers from or for both Birmingham and Jacksonville and beyond.

③ Sleeper open for occupancy at 9.30 PM.

Along with the *Dixie Flagler*, two other reserved-seat streamlined coach trains were inaugurated in December of 1940 to provide Midwest travelers with an economical alternative to Pullman service between Chicago and Florida. The *City of Miami* made its first run on December 18th, followed by the *South Wind* on December 19th. Three cooperating railroads—the Pennsylvania (PRR), Illinois Central (IC), and Chicago & Eastern Illinois (C&EI)—set up the three trains to operate in rotation every third day on a one-night out 29-1/2 hour service between Chicago-Jacksonville-Miami. By 1948, Pullman sleepers were added to the consists of the three trains. The *City of Miami* was routed over the IC (Chicago to Birmingham), CofG (Birmingham to Albany), ACL (Albany to Jacksonville) and FEC (Jacksonville to Miami). Motive power was provided by run-through IC diesels and its light-weight passenger equipment was in due course painted in the IC's standard paint scheme. IC E7-A No. 4009, having run through from Chicago with the *City of Miami*, joins the lineup of ACL E6-A Nos. 512, 516, 509 and 503 at the Jacksonville roundhouse on July 30, 1947.

(ACL Photo)

The schedule and equipment of the *City of Miami* on April 27, 1952.

Train No. 6, the northbound *South Wind*, nears Okeechobee, Florida (while being routed over the SAL during the FEC strike) in December of 1966. ACL E7-A No. 541 leads an A-A two-unit diesel consist during the last winter season of the trains' operation before the ACL-SAL merger. Note the ACL lightweight baggage car behind the locomotives and the leased Northern Pacific dome sleeping car, both familiar features of the trains' consist. The *South Wind* was routed over the PRR (Chicago to Louisville via Indianapolis), L&N (Louisville to Montgomery), ACL (Montgomery to Jacksonville) and FEC (Jacksonville to Miami). While the train is operating in this photo with a solid consist of ACL motive power, the ACL and PRR shared motive power and mixed ACL-PRR locomotive consists were frequently seen on the *South Wind*.
(David W. Salter Photo)

The ACL's southbound *South Wind* negotiates the crossovers as its departs Chicago's Union Station on the tracks of the Pennsylvania Railroad on July 2, 1966. Two E-8's, led by No. 556, pull the train of streamlined equipment on its 8:30 a.m. departure. Behind the diesels is a train of sleeper cars for Miami, Sarasota, St. Petersburg and Jacksonville; coaches for Miami, St. Petersburg, Sarasota and Naples; diners for Miami and Tampa; and, lounges for St. Petersburg and Tampa.
(Louis A. Marre Collection)

Far from its home rails, ACL E-6 No. 505 rolls the southbound *South Wind* at Clymers, Indiana on the tracks of the Pennsylvania Railroad on September 4, 1963. The *South Wind* operated southbound from Chicago via the Pennsylvania Railroad and northbound from points in Florida (Miami, St. Petersburg, Sarasota and Tampa) via the Florida East Coast Railway and ACL Railroad every other day in each direction.

(Louis A. Marre Collection)

The schedule and equipment of the *South Wind* on April 27, 1952.

SOUTH WIND

Southbound from Chicago via PRR:
April 29. May 2, 5, 8, 11, 14, 17, 20, 23, 26, 29. June 1, 4, 7, 10, 13, 16, 19, 22, 25, 28. July 1, 4, 7, 10, 13, 16, 19, 22, 25, 28, 31 and every 3rd day thereafter.

Northbound from Miami via FEC Ry:
April 27, 30. May 3, 6, 9, 12, 15, 18, 21, 24, 27, 30. June 2, 5, 8, 11, 14, 17, 20, 23, 26, 29. July 2, 5, 8, 11, 14, 17, 20, 23, 26, 29 and every 3rd day thereafter.

Southbound Read down	TABLE I	Northbound Read up
	Central Time	
9.00 AM	Lv **Chicago**..................PRR Ar	5.45 PM
12.40 PM	Lv Indianapolis.................." Ar	1.55 PM
3.00 PM	Lv **Louisville**.................." Ar	11.35 AM
6.32 PM	Lv Nashville...............L&N Ar	8.05 AM
10.22 PM	Ar Birmingham.................." Ar	4.15 PM
12.20 AM	Ar **Montgomery**.............." Ar	4.15 PM
12.30 AM	Lv Montgomery.................." Lv	2.25 AM
2.55 AM	Lv Dothan..................ACL Ar	2.15 AM
		11.40 PM
	Eastern Time	
5.55 AM	Ar Thomasville.................." Lv	10.50 PM
5.58 AM	Lv Thomasville.................." Ar	10.45 PM
7.51 AM	Ar Waycross (Oklahoma Ave.) " Ar	8.50 PM
9.25 AM	Ar **Jacksonville**.............." Lv	7.20 PM
9.45 AM	Lv **Jacksonville**.............." Lv	7.00 PM
10.21 AM	Ar St. Augustine...........FEC Ar	6.16 PM
11.15 AM	Ar Daytona Beach............." Lv	5.23 PM
11.35 AM	Ar New Smyrna Beach........" Lv	5.00 PM
12.35 PM	Ar Cocoa-Rockledge.........." Lv	3.56 PM
12.55 PM	Ar Melbourne.................." Lv	3.35 PM
1.28 PM	Ar Vero Beach.................." Lv	3.04 PM
1.47 PM	Ar Fort Pierce.................." Lv	2.49 PM
2.20 PM	Ar Stuart......................" Lv	2.19 PM
3.04 PM	Ar West Palm Beach.........." Lv	1.38 PM
3.17 PM	Ar Lake Worth................." Lv	1.22 PM
3.31 PM	Ar Delray Beach..............." Lv	1.08 PM
3.42 PM	Ar Boca Raton................." Lv	12.57 PM
4.05 PM	Ar Ft. Lauderdale............." Lv	12.36 PM
4.18 PM	Ar Hollywood................." Lv	12.24 PM
4.45 PM	Ar **Miami**..................." Lv	12.01 PM
① 9.50 AM	Lv Jacksonville................" Ar	
① 1.10 PM	Ar Orlando................ACL Ar	6.25 PM ①
① 2.40 PM	Ar Lakeland..................." Lv	2.50 PM ①
① 3.30 PM	Ar **Tampa**.................." Lv	1.28 PM ①
① 5.03 PM	Ar Bradenton................." Lv	12.40 PM ①
① 5.25 PM	Ar **Sarasota**.............." Lv	10.47 AM ①
① 9.50 AM	Lv Jacksonville................" Lv	10.30 AM ①
① 11.50 AM	Ar Gainesville................." Ar	6.30 PM ①
① 12.55 PM	Ar Ocala....................." Lv	4.18 PM ①
① 1.45 PM	Ar Leesburg................." Lv	3.07 PM ①
① 4.20 PM	Ar Clearwater................" Lv	2.10 PM ①
① 5.05 PM	Ar **St. Petersburg**........" Lv	11.50 AM ①
		11.15 AM ①

EQUIPMENT

Special Service Charge in Reserved Seat Coach. See Page 26.

Type of Car	Car No. Southbound	Car No. Northbound	Between	Accommodations
Coach	SW 6	SW 6	Chicago-Miami	36 Reclining, reserved seats
Sleepers	SW 43	SW 43	Chicago-Miami	6 Sec., 6 Dble Bedrooms
	SW 42	SW 42	Chicago-Miami	10 Roomettes, 6 Dble Bedrooms
	SW 41	SW 41	Chicago-Miami	6 Dble Bedrooms, Bar-Lounge
Diner Sleeper	SW 40	SW 40	Chicago-Jacksonville	10 Roomettes, 6 Dble Bedrooms
Coaches	SW 5	SW 5	Chicago-Jacksonville	52 Reclining, reserved seats
	SW 4	SW 4	Chicago-Miami	52 Reclining, reserved seats
	SW 3	SW 3	Chicago-Miami	52 Reclining, reserved seats
	SW 2	SW 2	Chicago-Miami	52 Reclining, reserved seats
Tavern-Lounge-Obs.			Chicago-Miami	

① — Via connecting train.

A predecessor train on the route used by the *South Wind* was the *Florida Arrow*, a Chicago to Florida winter train introduced on January 2, 1935. The seasonal tri-weekly *Florida Arrow* had a consist of heavyweight Pullman sleepers and coaches on its two-nights-out 35-hour run from Chicago to Miami. For a while the train featured Pullman's first lightweight sleeping car that had been exhibited at the 1933 World's Fair. In this photo, Miss *Florida Arrow* is shown with railroad officials and dignitaries at Chicago's Union Station about to christen the *Florida Arrow* before its maiden run to Florida. Note the Pennsylvania Railroad steam locomotive that will handle the train on the initial leg of its trip from Chicago to Louisville.

(ACL Photo)

In this publicity photo, shot for the inaugural ceremonies of the *Florida Arrow*, the Pennsylvania Railroad Conductor and young girl admire the Florida oranges that adorn the rear of the trains' tavern-lounge-observation car, along with palm branches and Spanish moss. The drumhead identified the *Florida Arrow's* cooperating railroads. The train served both coasts of Florida, offering through sleepers from Chicago, Indianapolis and Louisville to Miami and from Chicago to Sarasota and St. Petersburg. Through coaches were operated from Chicago to Jacksonville. The *Florida Arrow* did not operate during World War II, then returned for the 1946-47 winter season. It operated for the last time during the 1948-49 winter season.

(ACL Photo)

SEMINOLE

TABLE J

Southbound Read down		Central Time		Northbound Read up
5.10 PM	Lv Chicago	IC	Ar	10.30 AM
6.45 PM	Lv St. Louis	"	Ar	7.47 AM
12.18 AM	Lv North Cairo	CofGa	Ar	3.14 AM
9.00 AM	Lv Birmingham		Ar	6.05 PM
10.19 AM	Lv Sylacauga	"	Ar	4.42 PM
12.08 PM	Lv Opelika		Ar	3.05 PM
		Eastern Time		
2.15 PM	Lv Columbus	"	Ar	2.55 PM
4.30 PM	Ar Albany		Lv	12.55 PM
4.40 PM	Lv Albany	ACL	Ar	12.35 PM
5.45 PM	Ar Tifton	"	Lv	11.10 AM
7.25 PM	Ar Waycross (Plant Ave.)	"	Ar	9.30 AM
7.45 PM	Lv Waycross (Plant Ave.)	"	Ar	9.10 AM
9.10 PM	Ar Jacksonville		Lv	7.45 AM
9.10 PM	Lv Jacksonville	FEC	Ar	7.00 AM ②
⑩10.30 PM	Lv St. Augustine	"	Lv	6.11 AM ②
⑪11.07 PM	Ar Daytona Beach	"	Lv	5.03 AM ②
12.24 AM	Ar West Palm Beach	"	Lv	12.03 PM ②
4.47 AM	Ar Ft. Lauderdale	"	Lv	10.45 PM ①
6.07 AM	Ar Hollywood	"	Lv	10.28 PM ①
6.24 AM	Ar Miami	ACL	Lv	10.00 PM ①
7.00 AM			Lv	
⑩10.30 PM	Lv Jacksonville		Ar	6.30 AM ②
3.10 AM	Ar Orlando	"	Lv	12.15 AM ②
4.14 AM	Ar Haines City	"	Lv	11.57 PM ①
4.40 AM	Ar Lake Alfred	"	Lv	11.40 PM ①
5.50 AM	Ar Lakeland	"	Ar	10.30 PM ①
6.45 AM	Ar Tampa	"	Ar	7.10 PM ①
9.30 AM	Lv Tampa	"	Lv	5.03 PM ①
10.47 AM	Ar Bradenton	"	Lv	4.45 PM ①
11.30 AM	Ar Sarasota	"	Ar	9.35 PM ⑩
6.35 AM	Lv Haines City	"	Lv	8.51 PM ⑩
7.08 AM	Ar Lake Wales	"	Lv	7.55 PM ⑩
8.09 AM	Ar Sebring	"	Lv	6.00 PM ⑩
10.40 AM	Ar Clewiston	"	Ar	6.30 AM ⑩
⑩10.30 PM	Lv Jacksonville		Ar	10.25 PM ①
5.00 AM	Lv Lake Alfred	"	Lv	10.05 PM ①
5.25 AM	Ar Winter Haven	"	Lv	6.45 PM ①
9.20 AM	Ar Fort Myers	"	Ar	6.00 AM ②
⑩11.00 PM	Lv Jacksonville	"	Ar	3.20 AM ②
1.30 AM	Ar Gainesville	"	Lv	1.00 AM ②
3.45 AM	Ar Ocala	"	Lv	7.00 PM ②
9.35 AM	Ar Clearwater	"	Lv	6.15 PM ①
10.30 AM	Ar St. Petersburg	"		

EQUIPMENT

Type of Car	Car No. Southbound	North-bound	Between Accommodations
Coaches			Chicago-Jacksonville Reclining seats
			St. Louis to Carbondale Reclining seats Between all points
Cafe-Lounge			Chicago-Jacksonville
Sleepers	903	903	Chicago-Jacksonville 8 Sections, 2 Compts., 1 D. R.
	905	905	St. Louis-Jacksonville 8 Sec., 2 Compts., 1 D. R.
	S	S	Jacksonville-Miami 10 Sec., 2 Compts., 1 D. R.
	R508	R508	Jacksonville-Orlando 8 Sections, 2 Compts., 1 D. R.
	A 162	A 162	Jacksonville-Tampa 10 Sections, 1 Compt., 1 D. R.
	A 163	A 163	Jacksonville-Ft. Myers 10 Sec., 2 Compts., 1 D. R.

① Via connecting train.
② Flag stop to receive or discharge passengers.
⑩ Sleepers may be occupied until 7.00 AM.
⑪ Operates Mondays, Wednesdays and Fridays only.
⑫ Operates Tuesdays, Thursdays and Saturdays only.

Other famous Midwest-Florida passenger trains that plied the Illinois Central route were the *Seminole*, inaugurated in October of 1908, and the *Floridian*, inaugurated on December 7, 1922. Both trains had an evening departure from Chicago and offered a two-nights-out service to Miami. The *Floridian* originated during the 1920s Florida boom years and operated as a luxurious all-Pullman train with through sleeping cars to both coasts of Florida. The *Seminole* was the first train on the IC/CofG/ACL route to offer sleeping car service between Chicago, St. Louis and Florida. The *Seminole* also innovated the mid-train used of lounge cars during the 1930s and was noted for the Indian design on the drumhead of its section observation car. The northbound *Seminole* is shown here as it arrives at the ACL's passenger station at Orlando, Florida.

(ACL Photo)

The schedule and equipment of the *Seminole* on April 27, 1952.

Right: Through Pullman sleeping cars from Detroit and Cleveland for St. Petersburg and Miami were added to the *Southland* at Cincinnati. By the 1930s, the *Southland* was operating daily in two sections from Albany, Georgia. An east coast section operated via Albany to Jacksonville, then FEC to Miami with a dining car, Pullman sleeping cars and coaches. A west coast section operated from Albany via the Perry Cutoff route to Tampa and Sarasota with observation car, dining car, Pullman sleeping cars and coaches. After World War II, the *Southland* continued to operate east and west coast sections to Albany, but its east coast section began to be handled by the *Dixie Flyer* over the ACL to Jacksonville. Operation of the *Southland* came to an end in the late-1960s. In happier days, these travelers posed in the studio on a replica of the open platform of the *Southland's* 10-section observation car. Among those posing on the open platform is "Silver King", the famous movie dog from the silent screen era of motion pictures.

(ACL Photo)

In a classic view of a 1920s era ACL passenger train, Class P-5-A Pacific No. 1507 is shown passing Mile Post S-302 north of Inverness, Florida with Train No. 33, the southbound *Southland* in 1929. The train is on the double track line between Dunnellon and Trilby, Florida shortly after the completion of the Perry Cutoff north of Dunnellon between Perry and Monticello, Florida. When the Perry Cutoff was opened, it enabled the ACL to establish a new and considerably shorter passenger route from the Midwest to the West Coast of Florida. However, the *Southland* was the only passenger train that would operate on this route. The *Southland* operated on the PRR (Chicago to Cincinnati), L&N (Cincinnati via Knoxville to Atlanta), CofG (Atlanta to Albany) and ACL (Albany via Thomasville, Georgia over the Perry Cutoff to St. Petersburg, Tampa and Sarasota. The Southland was inaugurated on December 20, 1908 and initially operated between Chicago, Cincinnati and Jacksonville. Its new route was established after the Perry Cutoff was opened on December 4, 1928.

(ACL Photo)

SOUTHLAND

TABLE L

Southbound Read down			Northbound Read up
	Central Time		
11.35 PM	Lv Chicago................	PRR Ar	6.40 AM
	Eastern Time		
11.40 PM	Lv Detroit................	B&O Ar	
1.30 AM	Lv Toledo................	"	7.20 AM
5.15 AM	Lv Dayton................	"	5.30 AM
6.00 AM	Lv Hamilton..............	"	1.15 AM
8.00 AM	Lv Cincinnati............	"	12.35 AM
3.10 PM	Lv Knoxville.............	L&N Ar	9.25 PM
7.10 PM	Ar Atlanta...............	Ar	1.35 PM
8.00 PM	Lv Atlanta...............	Ar	9.25 AM
10.30 PM	Lv Macon.................	CofGa Ar	8.40 AM
1.00 AM	Ar Albany................	Ar	6.00 AM
1.15 AM	Lv Albany................	Lv	3.45 AM
2.50 AM	Ar Thomasville...........	ACL Ar	3.35 AM
3.00 AM	Lv Thomasville...........	"	2.00 AM
⑤ 6.54 AM	Ar Inverness.............	" Ar	1.50 AM ⑤
8.55 AM	Ar Tarpon Springs........	" Lv	9.44 PM
9.35 AM	Ar Clearwater...........	" Lv	7.35 PM
10.30 AM	Ar St. Petersburg........	" Lv	7.00 PM
9.15 AM	Ar Tampa................	" Lv	6.15 PM
9.30 AM	Ar Tampa................	" Lv	7.35 PM
10.47 AM	Ar Bradenton.............	" Ar	7.10 PM
11.30 AM	Ar Sarasota..............	" Lv	5.03 PM
⑥ 2.40 AM	Ar Ft. Myers.............	" Lv	12.45 PM ⑥
2.50 AM	Lv Albany................	"	
5.40 AM	Ar Waycross (Plant Ave.).	" Ar	2.00 AM
6.00 AM	Lv Waycross (Plant Ave.).	" Lv	11.00 PM
7.45 AM	Ar Jacksonville..........	"	10.45 PM
② 9.50 AM	Lv Jacksonville..........	" Lv	9.00 PM
② 11.51 AM	Ar DeLand................	" Ar	6.25 PM ②
② 12.43 PM	Ar Winter Park...........	" Lv	4.04 PM ②
② 1.10 PM	Ar Orlando..............	" Lv	7.00 PM ②
② 1.56 PM	Ar Haines City..........	" Lv	2.50 PM ②
② 2.40 PM	Ar Lakeland.............	" Lv	1.56 PM ②
② 9.50 AM	Lv Jacksonville..........	" Lv	1.28 PM
② 11.50 AM	Ar Gainesville...........	" Ar	6.30 PM ②
② 12.55 PM	Ar Ocala................	" Lv	4.18 PM ②
② 1.45 PM	Ar Leesburg.............	" Lv	3.07 PM ②
② 8.30 AM	Lv Jacksonville..........	" Lv	2.10 PM ②
② 9.06 AM	Ar St. Augustine........	FEC Ar	8.28 PM ②
② 10.00 AM	Ar Daytona Beach........	" Lv	7.40 PM ②
② 1.48 PM	Ar West Palm Beach......	" Lv	6.42 PM ②
② 2.48 PM	Ar Ft. Lauderdale.......	" Lv	2.41 PM ②
② 3.02 PM	Ar Hollywood............	" Lv	1.37 PM ②
② 3.30 PM	Ar Miami................	" Lv	1.23 PM ②
			1.00 PM

EQUIPMENT

Type of Car	Car No. South-bound	Car No. North-bound	Between Accommodations
Coaches			Chicago-Cincinnati Reclining seats
			Detroit-Cincinnati Reclining seats
			⑧ Cincinnati-Tampa Reclining seats
			⑧ Cincinnati-St. Petersburg Reclining seats
			Cincinnati-Jacksonville Reclining seats
			Between all points
Sleepers	B 100	B 100	⑧ Detroit-St. Petersburg 10 Sections, 2 Compts., 1 D. R.
	R 303	R 303	⑧ Chicago-St. Petersburg 8 Sections, 2 Compts., 1 D. R.
Diners			Serving all meals
Sleepers	R 302	R 302	⑧ Chicago-Tampa-Sarasota 8 Sections, 1 D. R., 3 Dble B. R.
	11	11	⑧ Atlanta-Tampa-Sarasota 8 Sections, Buffet-Lounge
	R 301	R 301	Chicago-Jacksonville 8 Sections, Buffet-Lounge

⑨ St. Louis passengers may use through coach and Pullman equipment on train 54-56 leaving Nashville 12.05 AM, arriving St. Louis 7.55 AM.
⑤ Sleeper may be occupied until 7.30 AM.
⑥ Sleeper open for occupancy 9.30 PM.

ATLANTIC COAST LINE
EASTERN TRAINS

	LEAVE TAMPA	DAILY
	...ST LINE MAIL	8.00 A.M.
	...PA SPECIAL	11.50 "
	...GNOLIA LIMITED	11.50 "
	...T COAST LIMITED	11.50 "
	...T COAST LIMITED	12.35 P.M.
	...METTO LIMITED	10.10 "
	...EVERGLADES	12.01 A.M.

...ROUGH PULLMAN CARS

THE SOUTHLAND

THE SOUTH...
DIXIE FLYE...
SEMINOLE...
ST. LOUIS E...
THE FLORID...
DIXIE LIMIT...
THE FLAMI...

THROUGH...

In a scene very much reminiscent of the old AB&C Railroad, ACL Atlanta-Waycross Local Passenger Train No. 101 is shown at Cordele, Georgia about the cross the GS&F (Southern Railway) and Seaboard Air Line Railway tracks. The photo was taken on September 20, 1947 in the year following the ACL's acquisition the AB&C. ACL Class AJ-1 light Pacific No. 7072 was formerly AB&C No. 72/former FEC No. 103.

(George B. Mock. Jr. Photo/David W. Salter Collection)

Top Right: One of the most interesting of the Western local passenger operations was the service between Atlanta and Waycross, Georgia on the former-AB&C Railroad. For many years, the AB&C had operated two daily local passengers between those points in the daylight hours as Train Nos. 1 and 2. Following the ACL acquisition of the AB&C on January 1, 1946, the trains were operated as ACL Train Nos. 101 and 102. In this photo, we see the ACL Atlanta-Waycross Local Passenger, Mail and Express Train south of Atlanta on September 2, 1946. Motive power is provided by ACL Class AJ-1 light Pacific No. 7075 (former AB&C No. 75/former FEC No. 110).

Bottom Right: The Atlanta-Waycross local Nos. 101 and 102 were popular with photographers because of their operation during daylight hours. No. 101 departed Atlanta Union Station at 9:15 a.m. and made the 279-mile run to Waycross at 5:45 p.m. Its counterpart, Train No. 102, departed Waycross at 9:35 a.m. and arrived Atlanta at 6:00 p.m. Operation of the locals was discontinued in 1958. In this view, Train No. 102, is shown at Gay, Georgia— west of Manchester— with a substantial consist of express business in March of 1954. The train is being handled by two FP7-A's, with No. 893 in the lead.

(Both: Richard O. Sharpless Photo/David W. Salter

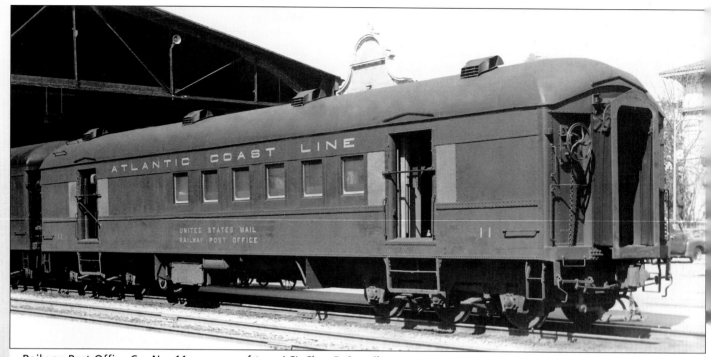

Railway Post Office Car No. 11 was one of two ACL Class D-6 mail cars. RPO No. 11, and its companion No. 12, were 64' 2" long and were built by Pullman for the ACL in 1926. The car was photographed at Augusta, Georgia in April of 1967.

(Al M. Langley, Jr. Photo)

This is an interior view of the mail sorting area of RPO No. 11 taken after it was remodeled in 1948. The improvements were designed to enhance the comfort and convenience of the mail clerks, thus facilitating their speed and accuracy in the handling of mail. Improvements included an enlarged wash room; a modernized heating system; modern double glazed windows with automatic screens; an improved lighting system with lights arranged scientifically and increased wattage; and, improved ventilation. The width of the car's side door openings was also increased, with radiator bulk heads cut down, giving much more room for loading and unloading mail bags.

(ACL Photo)

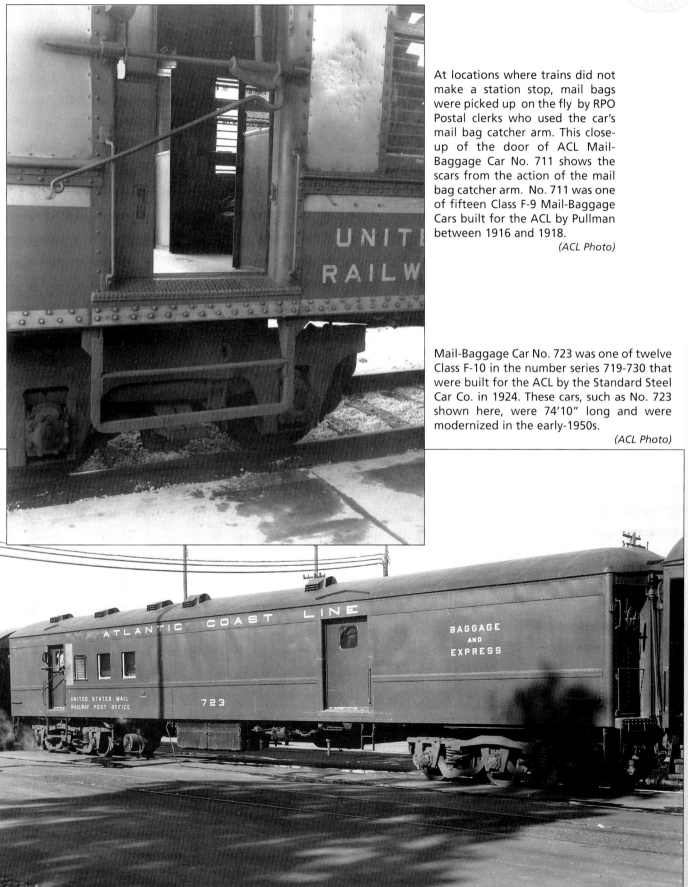

At locations where trains did not make a station stop, mail bags were picked up on the fly by RPO Postal clerks who used the car's mail bag catcher arm. This close-up of the door of ACL Mail-Baggage Car No. 711 shows the scars from the action of the mail bag catcher arm. No. 711 was one of fifteen Class F-9 Mail-Baggage Cars built for the ACL by Pullman between 1916 and 1918.

(ACL Photo)

Mail-Baggage Car No. 723 was one of twelve Class F-10 in the number series 719-730 that were built for the ACL by the Standard Steel Car Co. in 1924. These cars, such as No. 723 shown here, were 74'10" long and were modernized in the early-1950s.

(ACL Photo)

In 1926, the ACL purchased its last new mail-baggage cars. Also designated as Class F-10 and numbered in the series 731-735, these five cars were 74' 10" long and were built by Pullman. F-10 Mail-Baggage Car No. 734 is at the Rocky Mount shops on March 18, 1947.

(ACL Photo)

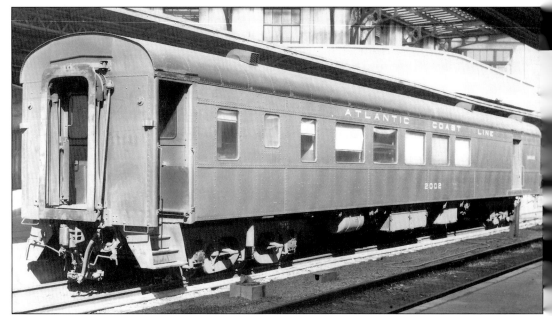

In 1947, the ACL acquired ten surplus army hospital cars from the United States government and converted six in the company shops to serve as baggage-dormitory cars on the best passenger trains. These cars were numbered in the series 2002-2007 and had bunk accommodations for 24 crew members. Baggage-Dormitory Car No. 2002 is at Broad Street Station in Richmond, Virginia on April 10, 1971.

(Tom King Photo/
C. K. Marsh, Jr. Collection)

ACL Class C-11 Express Car No. 582 was rebuilt from Coach 982 in 1950. The newly rebuilt car is shown on February 21, 1950 at the Emerson shops at South Rocky Mount, North Carolina.

(ACL Photo)

Top: The interior of Class C-11 Express Car No. 582 after being turned out at the Rocky Mount shops on February 21, 1950. The metal poles inside the car were used to provide bracing to stabilize boxes, crates, mail sacks and luggage that might be carried in the car.

Middle: All steel Class C-8 Express Car No. 1620 was built by Pullman-Standard in 1926.

Bottom: In 1947 and 1948, the ACL purchased fifty new, high-speed, express refrigerator cars from AC&F. Designated as Class CR and numbered in the series 3000-3049, the cars were designed to full passenger car standards and were operated in the fastest trains. Their overall length was 54'9" with a nominal capacity of 50 tons. They were the first of the ACL's rolling stock to be painted in the royal purple and aluminum paint scheme that was then being applied to its diesel locomotives. The cars had alternating royal purple and aluminum bands separated by yellow stripes. The lettering was painted aluminum and the roof, ends and under-body were painted black. The cars were repainted Pullman green with aluminum lettering in the late-1950s.

(All: ACL Photo)

Baskets of gladiolus flowers are loaded onto a new ACL Express-Refrigerator Car at Wilmington, North Carolina on July 8, 1948. These versatile "controlled temperature" cars were used in either refrigerator (under ice) or merchandise express traffic service.

(Both: ACL Photo)

The ACL owned a number of combination passenger-baggage cars such as Class E-11 Car No. 680 shown here in service in 1949. The Class E-11 cars were numbered in the series 671-680 and were built by Pullman-Standard in 1926. Four of the Class E-11 cars (677-680) were modernized for service on the *Vacationer*. The 680 is shown in its semi-streamlined appear-ance complete with side skirts as the result of the modernization rebuild at the ACL shops.

An interior view of the passenger section of Class E-11 Passenger-Baggage Car No. 680, taken at Florence, South Carolina on July 3, 1949.

(All: ACL Photo)

ACL Class A-15 Coach No. 1067 was one of fifteen in the number series 1065-1079 that were built in 1923-24 by the Standard Steel Car Company. The Class A-15 was the standard design for ACL heavyweight coaches and many were purchased by the railroad from various car builders between 1915 and 1926. The 1067 was a 83-foot coach originally with a seating capacity for 88 passengers. This was reduced to 54 after reclining seats were installed during a 1940s rebuild of the cars. Photographed in 1953, the 1067 was typical of the coaches operated on ACL passenger trains during the 1920s and 1930s.

An interior view of Class A-15 Coach No. 1057 taken on November 11, 1953 shows its straight back seats and ceiling fans. Built by Bethlehem Shipbuilding Corp. in 1923, Coach 1057 was a partitioned car with a seating capacity for 56 passengers. The car was later modernized with steam ejector type air conditioning and reclining seats. After its rebuild, the car had a women's lounge, one section with 42 reclining seats and another with 14 straight back seats.

Class A-15 Coach No. 1084 was the first in a series of heavyweight coaches to be modernized at the ACL's Emerson Shops at Rocky Mount, North Carolina. The coaches were completely stripped down and then rebuilt using the latest welding techniques and a minimum of rivets to give the exterior of the cars a smooth streamline appearance. The modernization of the cars consisted of installation of new spacious lounge rooms, re-spacing all side posts to accommodate large windows, applying turtle back roofs, closing up one vestibule, installing folding steps and rebuilding the ends to accommodate outside diaphragms. The cars also received modern electrical and air conditioning systems. *Inset*: The interior of modernized heavyweight Class A-15 Coach No. 1084. These were the first ACL cars to be constructed utilizing longitudinal lights under the bag racks as well as individual cross lighting. Modern rotating reclining seats have replaced the old style walk-over type seats. The original car had 88 seats while the new car had 54 seats, providing the passengers with greater comfort. Other new features included automatic door engines, illuminated car designation lights, modulating heat and cooling controls, and circuit breakers instead of fuses.

(All: ACL Photo)

By 1953, the Emerson shops had modernized twenty-three of the Class A-15 heavyweight coaches and they were assigned as follows: ten to Trains 75-76 (*Havana Special*); one to Trains 32-33 (*Southland* - Tampa to Cincinnati); two to Trains 38-32-33-37 (*Southland* - St. Petersburg to Cincinnati); six to Trains 77-78 (*Palmetto*); two to Trains 51-50 (Florence to Augusta);

and, two to Trains 48-49 (Wilmington to Rocky Mount). This view of Coach No. 1079 at Wilmington, North Carolina on September 17, 1953 shows the cars' full-width diaphragms

ACL heavyweight Dining Car the *Columbia* was built by Pullman-Standard in 1923. The car was 82' 4" in length, seated 36 and was in revenue service on the ACL until 1963. The car was photographed at Washington Terminal in Washington, D. C. in June of 1937.

(Harold K. Vollrath Collection)

Passengers dine aboard the ACL Dining Car the *Norfolk* in this view taken on February 27, 1930 at St. Petersburg, Florida. The *Norfolk* was 81'10" in length, seated 36 and was built for the ACL by Pullman-Standard in 1913.

(ACL Photo)

While most of the ACL's heavyweight dining cars seated 36 patrons, the railroad did some 48-seat dining cars. This is an interior view of the *Sanford*, a 83-foot, 48-seat dining car built new for the ACL by Pullman Standard in 1937.

(ACL Photo)

ACL Dining Car the *Kinston* was purchased second-hand from Pullman Standard in 1943. The car was 83'2" in length and seated 36 patrons. The dining car is at the Emerson shops in South Rocky Mount in 1950.

(ACL Photo)

This interior view of Parlor-Dining Car the *Goldsboro* shows the standard setup of linen, china and silverware in a late-1940s era ACL passenger train.

(ACL Photo)

Breakfast menu issued beginning July 2, 1958.

(K. L. Miller Collection)

ATLANTIC
CoastLine
RAILROAD

Club Breakfast

Please Write on Check "Club Breakfast" and Each Item Desired

CHOICE OF
Fruit, Fruit Juice or Cereal

SUGAR CURED HAM with Eggs (any style) 1.85
KIPPERED HERRING with Scrambled Eggs 1.75
EGGS (ANY STYLE) with Bacon Strips (3) 1.75
GOLDEN OMELETTE with Florida Guava Jelly 1.55
SELECTED FRESH COUNTRY EGGS, Boiled, Fried or Scrambled 1.35
* GRIDDLE CAKES with Bacon Strips (3) or Fried Eggs 1.75
BROWNED CORNED BEEF HASH with Poached Egg 1.65
* FRENCH TOAST with Syrup 1.25

Florida Orange Marmalade

Toast
Coffee   Tea   Corn Muffins
* Toast or Muffins Not Included.   Milk   Cocoa
Grits served with Club Breakfasts .15 Extra

A la Carte

Hot or Dry Cereals with Cream .50, with Sliced Banana .65
Fruit or Vegetable Juice .25
Chilled Melon .50   Florida Orange Juice .25   Double Juice .40
Stewed Prunes .40   Lemon Juice with Water .20   Sliced Florida Orange .25
Broiled Ham with Eggs 1.50   Individual Strained Honey .30
Broiled Bacon (6 Strips) 1.50, Half Portion (3 Strips) .85   Broiled Ham 1.50, Half Portion .90
Bacon 3 (Strips) with Eggs 1.50   Browned Corned Beef Hash with Poached Egg 1.50
Eggs—Boiled, Fried, Scrambled, Shirred (1) .50; (2) .80   Kippered Herring with Scrambled Eggs 1.50
Toast or Muffins .25   Hominy Grits .40   Eggs Poached on Toast (1) .55; (2) .85
Griddle Cakes or French Toast, Syrup or Honey .80; with Bacon Strips (3) 1.50
Coffee, Cocoa, Sanko, Postum, Tea .35   Plain Omelette .85
Omelette with Guava Jelly .95
Milk, Buttermilk .30

For Children ●

Parents may share their portions with children without extra charge.

WAITERS ARE NOT ALLOWED TO ACCEPT VERBAL ORDERS

An extra charge of 50 cents per person will be made for meals served out of dining car.
The States of Pennsylvania, North Carolina, South Carolina, Georgia and Florida
assess a Sales Tax of three per cent which must be collected from the buyer.

7-2-58   J. B. MASHBURN, Supt. Dining Cars
Atlantic Coast Line R. R. Co., Washington, D. C.

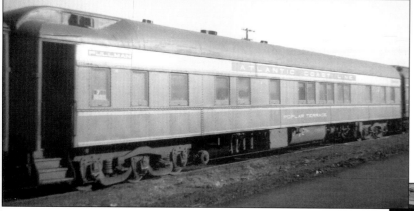

The ACL maintained a large fleet of heavyweight Pullman sleeping cars for service on the *Florida Special* and its other overnight trains. Most of these sleepers had either 8 or 10 sections with one drawing room and two compartments. Sleeping Car *Poplar Terrace*, at Albany, Georgia in October of 1962, had six sections and six double bedrooms. This car was built by Pullman in 1939 and was painted in an aluminum and purple paint scheme by the ACL in the early 1950s for service on the railroad's more important trains.

(C. L. Goolsby Collection)

Right: There was a dressing room for women in each sleeping car having section and berth accommodations. Its furnishings included a dressing table, chairs, wash basins and a generous number of mirrors. There was plenty of soap and hot water and ample supply of fresh towels. The toilet was in a separate annex.

(ACL Photo)

Bottom: Passenger-Baggage-Dormitory Car No. 107 was one of three such streamlined cars built by Budd for the ACL 1946. The car had a coach section that seated 20 passengers; another 26-foot section for baggage; and, a third section with bunk accommodations for 12 crew members. This car was later rebuilt to serve as a baggage-dormitory car that provided quarters for 33 crew members.

(ACL Photo)

The interior coach section of Passenger-Baggage-Dormitory Car No. 107 as it appeared on July 23, 1949.

(ACL Photo)

ACL lightweight Coach No. 216 was one of twelve streamlined coaches (216-227) built by Budd in 1946 for service on the *Champion*. Like all of the ACL's lightweight passenger equipment, they were equipped with roller bearings, four wheel trucks, a turtle back roof, tite-lock couplers, and anti-rattlers. Nine of the cars seated 54 passengers. The other three cars seated 46 passengers and had a section with sleeping quarters for the *Champion's* hostesses.

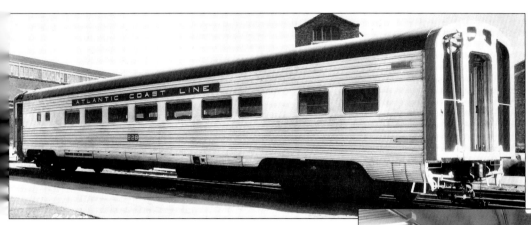

This interior view of an ACL 200-series lightweight coach shows the comfortable reclining seats, bulkhead murals with scenes of Florida, overhead lighting and large windows. Large, well-appointed dressing rooms were provided for both men and women at the opposite ends of the cars.

ACL Lightweight Coach No. 228 was one of twenty streamlined coaches (228-247) built by Pullman-Standard for the ACL in 1949. These coaches seated 54 passengers and allowed the ACL to operate some of the popular new lightweight equipment on the *Florida Special* and the *Vacationer*.

This closeup interior view of an ACL 200-series lightweight coach gives a detailed view of the amenities enjoyed by the passenger. These coaches were especially designed for overnight travel. The luxurious reclining chairs had linen headrests, individual arm rests and were located beside extra-wide picture windows and below individually controlled lights.

(All: ACL Photo)

Passenger Train Equipment

The *Baltimore* was one of three Budd dining cars built in 1940 for service on the *Champion*. The car was 85-feet long, seated 48 and had TP-56 trucks on the kitchen end and TP-55 trucks on the dining end. This is a kitchen side view of the car showing the service door that was used to stock the car with food and supplies.

(C. L. Goolsby Collection)

The Dining Car *Tampa* was built by Budd for the ACL in 1947. This car was also 85-feet long and seated 48 patrons. The kitchen end of the car is to the left in the photo, followed by the dining room area. Typical of the ACL lightweight cars, it had a purple letterboard, side skirts and a full-width diaphragm.

(ACL Photo)

The *Moultrie* was one of ten dining cars built by Pullman-Standard for the ACL in 1950. These 85-foot dining cars seated 36 and the service door was located between the kitchen and dining area rather than at the kitchen end of the car. This car has been restored to its ACL colors and name and operated by the Watauga Valley (Tennessee) Chapter NRHS.

(ACL Photo)

Right: This April 5, 1950 photograph shows the fully set dining room area of the Dining Car *Moultrie*.

Center Left: The train's Steward and his crew of waiters are ready for the evening meal aboard this ACL light-weight dining car. Announcements for meals were made over the train's public address system. Table d' hote meals and a la carte food were served in the train's dining cars.

Bottom Right: Cooks prepare another scrumptious meal for the ACL's passengers in the kitchen of this twin-unit dining car. The photograph was taken on July 7, 1951.

Bottom Left: A meal in a dining car was a memorable aspect of train travel. Patrons in the ACL dining cars could enjoy a la carte items such as hamburgers and specialty sandwich or table d' hoté dinners that including pan fried fillet of grouper, braised beef tips, broiled club steak or Florida fried shrimp.

(All: ACL Photo)

ATLANTIC
COAST LINE
RAILROAD

The Dining Car *Fitzgerald* is shown in the late-1960s after several modifications had been made to the car. This dining car was one of the ten 36-seat cars built by Pullman-Standard for the ACL in 1950. In this late 1960s, view, we see that the car has been modified with oval kitchen windows and the car has lost its purple letterboard and side skirts.

(C. L. Goolsby Collection)

Some of the 36-seat dining cars were set up as cafe lounge cars, with 24 cafe seats and 8 lounge seats. This interior view taken at Washington, D. C. on May 6, 1950 shows the cafe-lounge arrangement of the Dining Car *Plant City*. Other cars set up in a similar manner were the *Talladega, Cordele, Fitzgerald* and the *Tarboro*.

(ACL Photo)

On July 22, 1949, the first of 42 new ACL lightweight, streamlined, all-room sleeping cars departed New York in the *East Coast Champion*. Orders for the cars had been placed with Pullman-Standard in 1946 in conjunction with the Pennsylvania, RF&P and Florida East Coast railroads for use in interline service. However, the manufacture of the cars was delayed account the unavailability of labor and materials during the Second World War. Upon delivery, the cars were immediately assigned by the ACL to the two *Champions* and the *Miamian*.

(William E. Griffin, Jr. Collection)

Twenty-five of the new sleeping cars were 6 double bedroom-10 roomette sleeping cars named for counties in ACL territory. These 85-foot cars were part of a total postwar order for 74 lightweight, streamlined cars that were built by Pullman-Standard and Budd. The cars, such as the *Northampton County* shown in a builders photo, were of stainless steel construction and sported purple signboards. The ACL added four more 10-6 sleepers to its roster in 1950 when it purchased second-hand sleepers from the C&O.

(All: ACL Photo)

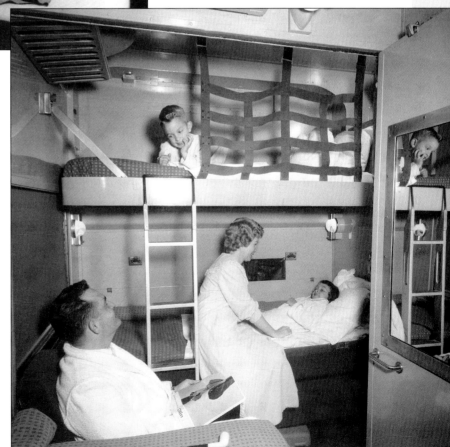

Above: Roomettes were designed for single occupancy and were arranged lengthwise in the sleeping car. Completely enclosed, the roomettes had their own toilets, washstands, clothes lockers and mechanically cooled drinking water. Lights, ventilation, air-conditioning and heating were controlled by the occupants of the room. For over-night travel, comfortable pre-made beds folded down from the wall. In this view through the window, the passenger has retired for the evening in her roomette.

Right: Connecting double bedrooms, divided by a sliding partition, could be connected into one large suite. In transverse bedrooms, which had a full length sofa, beds were arranged crosswise to the car. In longitudinal bedrooms, which had a contoured seat and folding chair, the beds were arranged lengthwise. Both rooms had full-size lower and upper beds. Each of the bedrooms accommodated two people and together, with the partition folded back, made an excellent accommodation for a family as shown in this photo.

Two young women enjoy their trip aboard an ACL sleeping car in a transverse double bed-room made up for day travel. At night, the full length sofa, which was positioned cross-wise to the car, folded out to make one of the beds. The other bed folded down from above the sofa. These ACL sleeping cars allowed passengers to enjoy a new standard of travel in their own private room.

(All: ACL Photo)

The *Ashley River* was one of six 14 roomette-2 drawing room sleeper cars built for the ACL by AC&F in 1949. However, the ACL soon found that the traveling public preferred the spacious bedrooms to the confined roomettes and in 1961 all of these cars were rebuilt and converted into 2 drawing room-7 double bed-room sleepers.

These new light-ed car numbering devices, seen here on a sleeping car, were installed on the ACL's light-weight passenger equipment.

The *Virginia Beach* was one of six 6 double bedroom-bar/lounge cars built for the ACL by AC&F in 1949.

(Both: ACL Photo)

This interior view of ACL 6 double bedroom-bar/lounge car *Ponte Vedra Beach* shows the bar/lounge section of the car.

The ACL owned 8 Tavern-Lounge-Observation cars in the number series 250-257, all originally purchased for use on the *Champions*. Tavern-Lounge Observation Car Nos. 250 and 251 were delivered by Budd in 1939 with rounded observation ends. One of these cars brings up the rear of the *Champion* near Jacksonville, Florida in the early days of the train's operation. The 250 was destroyed in a wreck at Milan, North Carolina in 1943 and the 251 was rebuilt by Budd in 1957 into a blunt-end car.

(All: ACL Photo)

Left: An interior view looking toward the rear section of an ACL rounded end Tavern-Lounge-Observation. The rear of cars 250 and 251 could seat 20 passengers in the lounge-observation section.

Another interior view of the observation section of an ACL rounded end Tavern-Lounge-Observation Car, this time looking toward the forward bulkhead end of the car.

This view of Tavern-Lounge-Observation Car No. 252 shows the car as it appeared in the late-1940s. The car had stainless steel signs with purple letterboards that wrapped around the ends. On the forward end, to the right in the photo, the car had a full-width diaphragm and the roof has been painted black. The car retains its skirts between the trucks.

(ACL Photo)

An interior view of the observation section of squared-end Tavern-Lounge Observation Car No. 254. These cars had a total seating capacity of 57 passengers, with 20 of the seats located in the observation lounge section.

(ACL Photo)

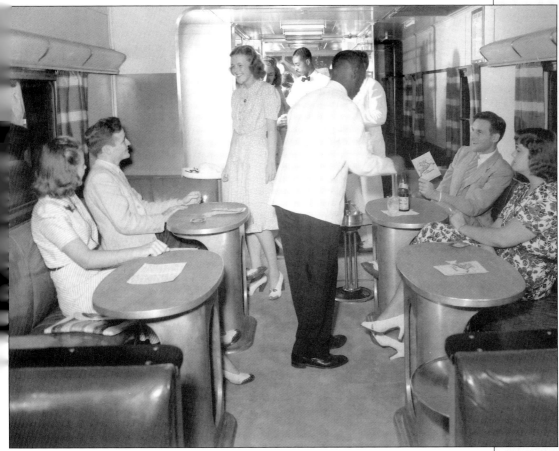

A bar was located in the middle of the Tavern-Lounge-Observation cars separating the observation and tavern sections. That bar section is discernible in this interior photo of the rear of the tavern section of the car. There was seating for 36 passengers in the tavern section. All of the Tavern-Lounge-Observation cars had fluorescent lighting and were air conditioned. The 1939 and 1940 cars had steam ejector air conditioning, while the 1947 cars had the more modern electromechanical air conditioning.

(ACL Photo)

ATLANTIC
COAST LINE
RAILROAD

"the only DOUBLE TRACK ROUTE BETWEEN THE EAST AND FLORIDA"

The ACL purchased six additional Tavern-Lounge-Observation cars from Budd. Three arrived in 1940 (Nos. 252-254) and the final three cars (Nos. 255-257) arrived in 1947. All six of these cars came with square-ends which permitted their use both in mid-train or rear-position assignments. While the more prevalent usage was mid-train, the cars were used on the rear of the train as shown in this photo of the *Champion* near Jacksonville, Florida in the early 1940s.

(ACL Photo)

FREIGHT SERVICE

Freight traffic became a significant source of revenue for the railroads that made up the "Atlantic Coast Line" when the "Atlantic Coast Despatch" was established in 1887. Prior to that time, freight traffic moving from the Southeast to New York and other Eastern points moved via the ACL's Wilmington and Weldon to Weldon, North Carolina, thence over the SAL's Seaboard and Roanoke to Portsmouth, Virginia and to its destination by steam boat. On August 1, 1887, a contract was signed by the Pennsylvania, RF&P, Washington Southern and the ACL (the Petersburg, the Richmond and Petersburg, and the Wilmington and Weldon) railroads to establish the "Atlantic Coast Despatch". Under this arrangement, the participating railroads agreed upon the rates, services and cars to be furnished by each for an all-rail line to New York and intermediate markets. Cars constructed for this service bore its name in a large oval. In this photo, ACL ventilated boxcar No. 39534, bearing the "Atlantic Coast Despatch" emblem, is being loaded at the Argent Lumber Company in Hardeeville, South Carolina in 1926.

(ACL Photo)

The development of the fruit and vegetable industry in Florida was influenced to a considerable extent by the availability of the fast all-rail service offered by the "Atlantic Coast Despatch". Prior to 1887, the Eastern markets had to rely on a slow rail/steam boat route and could only tap the farms of the Carolina coast for early vegetables and fruits. The development of the dedicated fast freight service over an all-rail route significantly improved the transit times for perishables and made pos-

sible the shipment of fresh fruits and vegetables from as far south as Florida. Within a year of the inception of the service, the movement of perishables had become a most important, albeit seasonal, source of revenue for the ACL. Certain perishables, such as watermelons, were successfully grown throughout the six states traversed by the ACL. These crops were of great economic importance to the South, providing income to the growers and employment to the people involved in their production, harvesting and marketing. These watermelons are being loaded during the summer of 1945 into ACL boxcars that have been spotted on a sidetrack in Georgia—then the premier watermelon producing state in the nation.

(ACL Photo/William E. Griffin, Jr. Collection)

6

While the ventilated boxcars and expedited transit times offered by the Atlantic Coast Despatch were suitable for the transportation of many fresh vegetables, they were still inadequate when it came to the proper shipment of certain fruits. To meet the demands of shipping these perishables railroads developed the refrigerated rail car. These early refrigerated cars were equipped with ice bunkers to cool the fruits and vegetables during their trip to market with the cars re-iced at various points en route in order to maintain the required temperature. Development of the refrigerated rail car, coupled with fast, dependable rail service enabled Florida growers to market their vegetables and fruit to a nationwide market. The shipment of strawberries from Florida to the eastern markets would not have been possible without refrigeration for few fruits are more perishable than strawberries. In this photo, ice is being loaded into the bunkers of Pennsylvania Railroad/American Railway Express cars at Plant City, Florida in 1930.

(Both: ACL Photo)

With the bunkers of the express cars fully iced, the Florida strawberry growers arrive at the ACL's Plant City, Florida facility where the berries are unloaded from their trucks and are packed and loaded for rail shipment.

While refrigerated rail cars had proved to be essential in the movement of certain perishables, these cars posed problems for the railroads. Given the seasonal nature of the perishable business, railroad companies had no desire to own and maintain a fleet of such equipment. This led to the creation of railway refrigerator express car companies. One such company was the Fruit Growers Express, Inc. that owned and operated refrigerator cars and facilities for the movement of perishables from the southern producing territory to the northern markets. This express company retired from the service in 1920 and the railroad companies principally concerned with the business organized the Fruit Growers Express Company, which took over the equipment and other property used for this traffic. The participating railroads subscribed to the stock of the new company on the basis of refrigerator car mileage over their respective roads. ACL Class E-4 0-6-0 No. 1140 is shown switching various ventilated and refrigerated cars, including those of the Fruit Growers Express and Western Fruit Express companies.

(Both: ACL Photo)

The peak freight traffic season for the ACL was during the winter months when perishables were moved to the northern markets. Much of this business was moved from Southern Florida via the Florida East Coast Railway and then interchanged with the ACL at Jacksonville. Perishable business also originated at various eastern locations on the ACL and was marshaled at Sanford, Florida for subsequent forwarding to Jacksonville. Perishable business on the west coast of Florida

was gathered up at locations such as Sarasota and Fort Myers and then assembled at Tampa and Lakeland for movement to Waycross, Georgia. The principal icing stations on the ACL were located at Sanford, Jacksonville, Waycross and Florence. This is a view of the new icing facility at Rands Yard, Sanford, Florida. Note the Atlantic Coast Despatch boxcars on the adjacent track.

The icing of refrigerator car bunkers was a labor intensive function, providing laborers with a good deal of seasonal employment at the railroad's many facilities in the South that serviced these cars. Images such as this began to disappear from the railroad scene after the 1950s when modern all-steel mechanically refrigerated boxcars replaced the old ventilated reefers.

(ACL Photo)

Class R-1 4-8-4 No. 1809 storms through South Richmond, Virginia with a northbound perishable train. At Richmond, the train will be interchanged with the RF&P for its run to Potomac Yard at Alexandria, Virginia. To enable its shippers to sell their products on the best market available, the ACL allowed cars to be simply waybilled to Waycross, Georgia for diversion. There they were iced and held until a market could be found in the North. Upon receipt of diversion instructions, the car or cars were placed in one of the regular perishable trains leaving Waycross for eastern or midwestern markets and moved through to destination. Waycross was an extremely active terminal during the season of peak perishable shipments from January to April. In later years, the ACL refined its diversion system to allow cars originating on the main line between Lakeland, Orlando and Jacksonville to be diverted at Jacksonville. Cars for eastern markets were then operated in regular trains via the Jesup short line, bypassing Waycross altogether.

(J. I. Kelly Photo)

Rolling past Mile Post 756, FT No. 302 heads up an extra northbound perishable train. The completion of double-tracking on the Jacksonville to Richmond main line and the addition of new locomotives and cars enabled the ACL to begin offering fourth-morning service to many northern markets in 1930. Following the Second World War, the increased operating efficiencies resulting from diesel locomotives, improved roadway and better signaling enabled the ACL to offer a vastly improved and more dependable fourth-morning service with extended loading times in Florida and earlier arrival times in the North. The ACL was also able to offer an even faster third-morning operation to New York City and intermediate points when warranted by the volume of traffic.

(ACL Photo)

In the first half of the twentieth century, the ACL practically lived during the winter months on the revenues it derived from Florida citrus fruit and vegetables, as well as the Florida tourist travel, and had to struggle through the summer months with a limited volume of business. Revenues came from the transportation of agricultural products such as cotton and tobacco, as well as livestock, which were the principal means of livelihood in the South. This changed after the Second World War when the Southeastern United States experienced an economic renaissance. The industrial growth of the South (three-fourths of the new plants were built in the postwar years from 1946 to 1953) resulted in a healthy diversification in the ACL's mix of traffic. One of the ACL's important new sources of freight revenue was derived from the transportation of forest products. A number of pulp and paper mills located on the railroad, and to move the increased pulpwood traffic, the ACL built, bought and leased thousands of additional cars in the post war era. Pulpwood cars, such as the ACL cars in this photo, were a common sight on side tracks and team tracks throughout the South.

(ACL Photo)

An unusual agricultural product transported by the ACL was sugar cane. The cane was grown on the Benbow Farm located south of Moore Haven, Florida near Lake Okeechobee. This farm was owned by the Southern Sugar Mill Company, which operated its own industrial railroad to move the harvested cane from the fields to a connection track with the ACL. The ACL then short-hauled the cars to the sugar processing mills at Clewiston, Moore Haven and South Bay.

(ACL Photo)

The ACL served no coal mines directly. Hence, all of the coal that it transported was received from its connecting lines. However, during the post-war period, the ACL's transportation of coal also increased as the railroad benefited from the dramatic growth of the economy in the Southeast. This increase in coal tonnage resulted from the construction and expansion of coal burning electric power plants in the South. To handle this new traffic, the ACL purchased more than 1200 new coal hopper cars between 1946 and 1953. Two 4-6-2's, with P-5-B No. 1604 in the lead, are required for this southbound freight of hopper cars. The train is north of Cordele, Georgia in September of 1948.

(David W. Salter Photo)

In the post-war era, the products of mines became a most important commodity in the ACL's mix of freight traffic. In fact, by 1954 the ACL was receiving nearly half of its freight tonnage and a fourth of its freight revenue from this source. Shipments of sand and gravel, stone and rock from quarries and pits in all of the states served by the ACL increased sharply, reflecting the need of these materials for construction of industries and roads in the South. Of even greater importance to the ACL, was the expansion of fertilizer and chemical industries in the South, resulting in a dramatic increase in the shipment of phosphate rock. The ACL served the richest phosphate rock producing area in the country centered primarily in Florida's Polk and Hillsborough counties. Large deposits of phosphate were first discovered in the bed of the Peace River in 1885 and commercial production began in 1888. Then in the 1890s, the early phosphate miners moved to the pebble fields.

The ACL moved wet rock in special type open-top hopper bottom-drop discharge rail cars to drying plants. It also transported dried rock in special covered-hopper bottom discharge rail cars from the mines to Port Tampa for water movement. In this 1930s view, the ACL tugboat *Neptune* is shown towing the ship *Laurac*, loaded with phosphate, at Port Tampa.

(ACL Photo)

ACL F7A No. 377 departs Tampa's Uceta Yard with a train of hopper cars on another trip to the Bone Valley pebble phosphate district on January 12, 1963. The Bone Valley district ranged over a 2,000 square mile area east of Tampa and was blanketed by a network of ACL tracks leading to nearly all of the mining areas and phosphate processing installations. The ACL's lines also connected the mining area with fertilizer and chemical manufacturing plants along Florida's west coast immediately east and south of Tampa and with the ACL's own phosphate elevator at Port Tampa. By the 1960s, the ACL owned more than 6,000 covered hopper cars assigned to the phosphate service and operated approximately 30 phosphate trains each day, handling 18,000 carloads each month.

(Barry Young Photo)

By the early 1950s, the increased revenues from the products of mines offset the losses in revenue that the ACL was beginning to experience from the transportation of perishables. The long distance trucking of Florida citrus fruits increased following the war and, by 1953, railroads were carrying only 52 percent of the total shipped to market as compared to 93 percent during the 1945-46 season. There was a corresponding loss in revenue. Whereas the ACL had received nearly 22 percent of its total freight revenue from the transportation of perishables in 1938, it was only collecting about 7 percent from that

source in 1953. Early in the 1960s, the ACL participated with three other companies (suppliers and builder) to develop a new freight car in an effort to capture more business from both the product of mines and products of agriculture . In 1964, the ACL introduced the "Whopper Hopper", at that time the largest car of its type in the world. In this publicity photo, four young ladies demonstrate its versatility by pouring bags of sugar, grain, fertilizer and phosphate into the car's four separate compartments.

(ACL Photo/William E. Griffin, Jr. Collection)

The "Whopper Hopper", shown here in service on the ACL, was a publicity success but an operational disappointment. Its water cleaning system was complicated and expensive to maintain and, the ACL found little demand for its capability to simultaneously transport different types of lading. The car remained in service into the 1990s, but was a one-of-a-kind piece of rolling stock. The ACL did not order any more of the jumbo hoppers.

(ACL Photo)

One innovative rail service that did prove to be successful was the operation of TOFC, or "Trailer-on-Flatcar", also commonly called "piggyback". This service involved the transportation of highway trailers on railroad flatcars and it gave railroads some of the pick-up and delivery flexibility that was enjoyed by truckers. It was also an economic long-haul option and enabled railroads to recapture some of the business that had been lost to truckers during the early post-war era. The ACL's first operation of TOFC service came in June of 1959 when trailers were loaded at the RF&P"s Potomac Yard in Alexandria, Virginia and were handled over the RF&P and ACL to Jacksonville, Florida. In later years, trailers would be lifted onto and off the rail cars by giant forklifts, called "piggypackers". In the beginning of the operation, trailers were loaded and unloaded via the use of ramps, with the trailers driven on and off the flatcars. This photo depicts an early ramp operation. The trailer has been ramped onto the rail car and is being positioned to be secured in place before the cab is uncoupled and driven off the car.

(ACL Photo)

TOFC was so successful that by the early-1960s, the ACL was offering the service between more than 125 points in the Southeast and other parts of the country. Loading ramps were constructed at 20 locations and the ACL operated a fleet of specially equipped flatcars and trailers that allowed it to offer shippers all of the established plans for operation of piggyback service. The ACL handled the trailers of the largest motor carriers in the Southeast and put into operation a complete door-to-door service with its own trailers. The ACL's trailers, shown here on a flatcar, were of aluminum construction with a large cargo capacity and carried the slogan "Thanks for Using Coast Line Piggyback Service". Fruit Growers Express Company also supplied a number of new refrigerated trailers to recapture from truckers the transportation of Florida citrus fruit that was being processed at local plants and shipped as canned juice, either in single strength or as a frozen concentrate. The ACL's first solid piggyback train departed from Lakeland on January 7, 1961, operating over the ACL, RF&P and Pennsylvania railroads with 39 cars in 32 hours between Florida and New York. The dedicated piggyback train would be a common sight on the ACL during the 1960s.

(ACL Photo)

Modified Class K-5-S "copperhead" 4-6-0 No. 989 rolls a short freight train at Scranton, north of Walterboro, South Carolina in an early-1920s photo that was taken prior to the double tracking of the Jacksonville to Richmond main line. Note the brakeman riding atop a boxcar mid-train, a hazardous operating practice that would eventually be outlawed by the railroads. Handling tonnage on the Northern Division between Richmond and Savannah posed no problems for the ACL and even K-5 Tenwheelers such as the 989 could handle 2470 tons in either direction when temperatures were above 30 degrees. Tonnage rating were reduced during the winter months.

(ACL Photo)

As a result of the easy grades on its main line between Richmond and Jacksonville, the ACL was unique among American railroads in its use for many years of the Pacific type steam locomotive as its standard motive power for both passenger and freight service. Fast freight service was handled by the P-5-B Class 4-6-2's in the 1600 and 1700 number series. These locomotives were rated at 4400 tons north of Savannah, and with 69-inch drive wheels, were capable of running at a maximum speed of 70 mph. Flying the flags of an extra freight, P-5-B Pacific No. 1665 storms out of Rocky Mount, North Carolina with a southbound freight in 1949.

(Mallory Hope Ferrell Photo)

As the lengths of both freight and passengers trains increased, as well as the weights of their rolling stock and lading, the ACL found it increasing necessary to resort to the expensive operating practice of doubleheading its Pacific steam locomotives in order to maintain train schedules. Photographer George B. Mock, Jr. captured this splendid portrait of double-head steam operation at Mock, just east of Albany, Georgia on the Albany-Waycross line on July 12, 1947. Two P-5-B Class 4-6-2's (Nos. 1644 and 1708) speed past with Train No. 504's long string of merchandise traffic.

(George B. Mock, Jr. Photo/David W. Salter Collection)

Top: Following the First World War, the ACL commenced a seven-year rehabilitation program to double track its main line between Richmond and Jacksonville. This project involved the installation of 131-pound rail, widened ditches for improved drainage, realignment to reduce excessive curvature, and the modernization and respacing of signals. Center pass tracks usually held 90 cars and determined the car limit of the majority of the freight trains during the steam era. When completed in 1925, the ACL had a north-south race track with low maintenance costs for the fast operation of both freight and passenger trains. Sometime after completion of the double tracking of the main line, the ACL dispatched one of its company photographers to photograph the finished project. Here, in an almost perfect scene captured by that unknown photographer is P-5-B Pacific No. 1672 with an extra freight near Natal, North Carolina.

Bottom: As P-5-B Pacific No. 1672 passed with its train, the company photographer turned to capture this going-away view. No doubt he went home pleased to have completed this assignment to record the ACL's new double track main line completely relaid with 131-pound rail, reballasted with crusted stone and retimbered with new cross ties, and with wide cuts that allowed for improved drainage from the railroad's right-of-way. He also produced two classic views of a typical ACL freight train from the 1920-30s era.

(Both: ACL Photo)

To avoid the doubleheading and change of its Pacific locomotives on the Richmond-Jacksonville main line, the ACL experimented in 1938 with the most modern steam locomotive the railroad would ever own—twelve R-1 Class 4-8-4 engines. Initially assigned to passenger assignments, they could handle twenty car passenger trains and maintain the schedule of the fastest runs, operating without change of power over the 648 miles between Richmond and Jacksonville. When the ACL dieselized the motive power of its passenger trains after the Second World War, the R-1 s were reassigned to main line freight service and performed admirably until retired and scrapped in the early-1950s. Here we see one of the R-1's speeding past the tower and station, and across the main line tracks of the Seaboard Air Line Railway, at Callahan, Florida with a southbound freight train for Jacksonville.

(William E. Griffin, Jr. Collection)

With the U.S. Highway 280 overpass in the background, Class M-S 2-8-2 No. 807 coasts through Musselwhite, just south of Cordele, Georgia on the afternoon of January 3, 1948 with a southbound local freight train. The ACL operated many local freights as the railroad originated or terminated about 90 percent of all its freight tonnage. More than one-third of the ACL's freight tonnage was both originated and terminated on-line. While a high percentage of the ACL's local tonnage was primarily the heavy movements of commodities like phosphate rock, sand, gravel and pulpwood, the local traffic also included boxcar traffic such as packaged food products and paper board.

(David W. Salter Photo)

M-2 Class 2-8-2 No. 812 is shown about to pass under the Bankhead Highway overpass as it arrives at Atlanta, Georgia on the afternoon of June 5, 1948 with a northbound extra freight. A gateway to western traffic, Atlanta was served by the ACL's Western District.

(David W. Salter Photo)

The busiest freight line on the ACL's system was the double track main line between Jacksonville and Richmond. Via its connection with the RF&P Railroad at Richmond, traffic routed over this line reached the Potomac Yard gateway to the East and West. Via its connection with the Florida East Coast Railway at Jacksonville, the ACL was able to serve the east coast of Florida. In this view, two new FT diesels are shown  departing Moncrief Yard at Jacksonville with a perishable train in 1944. The Southern Division route between Waycross, Georgia and the western gateway of Montgomery, Alabama, also carried heavy traffic. Two other outlets to the West, Atlanta and Birmingham, were on the Western Division, which principally served as a bridge line between those gateways and Florida and other portions of the Southeast served by the ACL. Other important interchange points were located at Augusta and Albany, Georgia; Columbia and Yemassee, South Carolina; Wadesboro, North Carolina; and, Norfolk and Petersburg, Virginia.

(ACL Photo)

F7 No. 395 heads up a consist of twelve cab units on a long southbound freight at Jesup, Georgia on April 28, 1961. It is doubtful that all units were "on line" as the ACL was most likely using this train to transfer motive power. The Nahunta Cut-off between Folkston and Jesup, Georgia, bypassing Waycross, was built in 1902 to shorten the route between Savannah and Jacksonville. In November of 1949, a new second track from Folkston to Newell, Georgia was placed in service to extend the ACL's double track northward from Folkston along the Jesup short line to relieve some of the traffic congestion of trains at Folkston during the winter season. Folkston was an important junction north of Jacksonville where tracks over which trains from Chicago and the Midwest converged with the ACL's double track main line for the New York-Florida traffic. In terms of the number of trains operated daily, the double track segments between Jacksonville and Folkston, and between Rocky Mount and Contentnea, North Carolina were the busiest portions of the ACL's system.

(Bruce R. Meyer Photo)

Top Right: Six F units, led by F7 No. 373, pull by the passenger station at Rocky Mount, North Carolina as they arrive with southbound freight train No. 109 in January of 1963. The ACL established Train No. 109 in March of 1954 to operate as a fast, through freight from Richmond to Jacksonville. The train actually originated at the RF&P's Potomac Yard in Alexandria, Virginia, where it was made up of shipments from New York and other eastern and midwestern origins. Received in interchange from the RF&P at Acca Yard in Richmond, the ACL operated No. 109 as a first class train from Acca to Jacksonville on a strict schedule only two hours behind that of its passenger train, the *Everglades*. There were no drag freights on the ACL. The average top operating speed was 60 mph for unrestricted loads and 50 mph for restricted loads. Train No. 109 made set outs of pre-blocked cars at Rocky Mount for North Carolina points; at Florence for South Carolina and southeastern destinations; at Southover Yard (Savannah) for southeastern points and the west coast of Florida; and, at Jacksonville for eastern and central Florida.

(Curt Tillotson, Jr. Photo)

Bottom Right: ACL Northbound Train No. 210, led by F7 No. 376 and three other F units, traverses Halifax Road crossing and is about to pass over the tracks of the Norfolk and Western Railway's belt line, as it departs Collier Yard at Petersburg, Virginia in July of 1966. To the right, an ACL switcher handles a delivery of interchange cars to the N&W at Seacoast. Petersburg's Collier Yard was not a large yard on the ACL system, however, it was the point of interchange for important traffic with the N&W.

(William E. Griffin, Jr. Photo)

While much of the ACL system was a double track water level route, there were exceptions. In addition to hilly country on the AB&C and C&WC, stiff grades were also found on the lines into Lakeland, Florida, the Montgomery District and the west end of the Waycross District. Westbound grades were particularly stiff on that portion of the Montgomery District west of Dothan and east of Troy, Alabama. The ACL assigned its largest steam locomotives to these areas. When diesel manufacturers began to offer high-horsepower six-axle locomotives in the early-1960s, the ACL acquired a number of the second generation diesels for service on the its lines west of Waycross. GE 2500-horsepower U25C No. 3000, two Alco C-628s, and two GP diesels roll their long freight train over the Georgia countryside on the single track line near Valdosta, Georgia in 1964.

Every thing comes to a stop in Valdosta, Georgia as Train No. 213 roars through town on June 14, 1964 with U25C No. 3002 and two Alco C-628's using their combined 8000-horsepower to power the 100-car train. The Southern Division route between Waycross and Montgomery carried heavy tonnage and, like the other important ACL routes, had one and in some cases two hotshot freight schedules daily in each direction. Phosphate rock and perishable trains from the Tampa area connected with the Waycross-Montgomery line at Dupont, Georgia. A important gateway for western traffic at Albany, Georgia was also reached off the Waycross-Montgomery line at Thomasville, Georgia.

(Both: Felix Brunot Photo/Robert H. Hanson Collection)

The ACL agent engages in some last minute conversation with the crew as the local freight departs Hobgood, North Carolina behind GP-7 No. 239 in May of 1966. The train is No. 514, the eastbound side of Local Freights 515/514 that operated between South Rocky Mount, North Carolina and Pinners Point, Virginia. The ACL also worked locals out of South Rocky Mount via Parmele, North Carolina on branch lines to Plymouth, Washington and Kinston, North Carolina. The ACL did have numerous branch lines, a situation that created financial headaches for the railroad as truck competition rendered some of the lines unprofitable. As a result, the ACL closed down a number of its branch lines, but only after a study had concluded that the line either could not feed valuable traffic to the main line or had lost the ability to make a profit on its own.

(Tom G. King Photo/C. K. Marsh, Jr. Collection)

The ACL controlled or had a large stockholder interest in a group of affiliated short line railroads, including the Columbia, Newberry & Laurens; the Winston-Salem Southbound; and, the Charleston and Western Carolina. The C&WC, which operated between the low country and Piedmont sections of South Carolina, via Augusta, Georgia, was merged into the ACL system in 1959. When the ACL acquired affiliated roads such as the AB&C and the C&WC, it was required to operate properties with curvatures and ruling grades vastly different from the ACL's main line along the Atlantic seaboard. To traverse the former-C&WC's Piedmont section with a long freight train, the ACL had to "beef up" the motive power to handle the tonnage. That's exactly what we see in this case, as GP-7 No. 265 and six cab units roll past in August of 1964 with a long merchandise freight at Simpsonville, South Carolina, on the former C&WC line between Laurens and Greenville, South Carolina.

(Jim Shaw Photo)

FREIGHT EQUIPMENT

ACL O-15 class ventilated and insulated box car No. 43766 is at Tampa, Florida in 1930. Stenciled for the "Atlantic Coast Despatch", the Class O-15 boxcars (number series 43735-44234) were built by the Baltimore Car & Foundry in 1921 and were patterned after USRA boxcars. These wooden boxcars had steel ends and a screen door that was used during warm weather when transporting vegetables or fruits.

(Both: ACL Photo)

ACL 0-17 class wooden ventilated boxcar No. 17397 is at Florence, South Carolina on September 5, 1957. Restenciled with the ACL logo, the O-17 cars (number series 17000-18999) were built in 1922 and 1923.

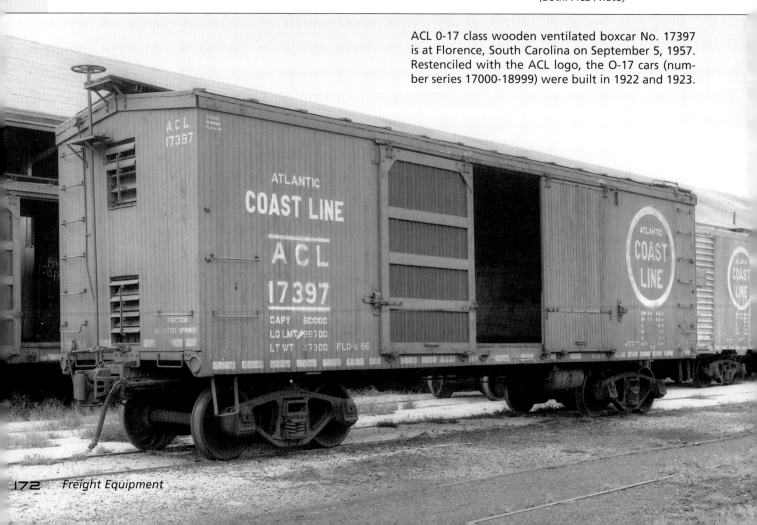

7

The hand brake end of wooden ventilator boxcar No. 17397, also photographed at Florence, South Carolina on September 5, 1957. The O-17 cars had a steel underframe and weighed 46,500 pounds. Fourteen of the Class O-17 boxcars were still on the ACL roster in 1965.

(ACL Photo)

ACL 50-ton 40-foot steel sheathed wood lined box car No. 21011 was a member of the Class 0-25 (number series 2000-21629). Nos. 2000-20799 were built by AC&F; 20800-21629 by Pullman Standard, all in 1942.

(ACL Photo)

ACL Class O-26 boxcars were numbered in the series 21630-23429 and were built by AC&F in 1949. The O-26 cars were 50-ton all steel wood lined boxcars with a single door. No. 21720 was selected for the builder's photograph of the class. In 1963, a number of the O-26 boxcars were outfitted to handle bulk and bagged phosphate. All lining was removed from the inside of the car and at the bottom of the floor a strip of metal was used to prevent damage by pay-loaders. An identifying "P", marking the special box cars, was painted in yellow on a green door.

(ACL Photo)

The Class O-16-D boxcars, numbered in the series 27000-27479, and the O-16-E boxcars, numbered in the series 27480-28133, were rebuilt at the ACL shops in 1943-1944 from boxcars formerly in the number series 47000-50699. This side view of Class O-16-D 40-ton all steel single door box car No. 27331 was taken in 1943.

(ACL Photo)

The ACL owned 100 Class O-16-F boxcars numbered 28200-28299. These cars were rebuilt by the ACL shops in 1939-1940 from boxcars formerly in the series 55000-57499. These all steel wood lined single door boxcars were equipped with Hyatt roller bearings and the whole class received heavy repairs at Waycross in 1953. Class O-16-F No. 28216 is at Waycross in 1965. The car displays the "Prismo" side and end stripes applied to cars painted in the company shops from 1951 to 1958.

(ACL Photo)

Between 1956 and 1957, AC&F built 500 Class O-30 (numbered 30000-30499) 50-foot single door boxcars for the ACL. The 50-ton cars were of all steel construction including the frame, floor and roof and had reinforced wood lining on the inside. Built to ACL specifications, the cars were equipped with roller bearings, had wide 9-foot doors and were designed to withstand heavier loads for long distance travel. These cars had additional braces welded into the end corrugations and corners for increased rigidity and were equipped with rubber cushioned draft gears to eliminate the shock and bumping cars receive when coupled together in yards. A freshly painted Class O-30 No. 30417 is at Waycross with the new ACL emblem and catchphrase "Another Cushioned Load". This new emblem was adopted and applied to equipment beginning in 1955. The familiar circle with the words, Atlantic Coast Line, was still there, but with a change in emphasis. In keeping with the company's general tendency to refer to the railroad as "Coast Line", the word, Atlantic, was made smaller and the words, Coast Line, were made larger in the same type of modern Gothic lettering that was currently being used in the ACL's general advertising.

(ACL Photo)

"Thanks For Using Coast Line" was another slogan used on the sides of ACL's boxcars. Conventional steel 50-foot boxcar No. 32351 was one of 135 Class O-33 single door cars in the number series 32350-32484 that were built in 1962 by Pullman-Standard. These boxcars were equipped with roller bearings, nailable steel floors and lading band anchors.

(ACL Photo)

No. 33000 was a one of a kind class of boxcar designed and put in service by the ACL in 1966 for general use by shippers requiring a first class car for various kinds of freight. Designated as Class O-37, the 33000 was a single-sheathed boxcar with no wood lining and the side posts that framed the car were on the outside of the car instead of between the hull and the inside lining. The prototype car was equipped with large 9-foot sliding doors, a smooth and easily cleaned interior, and cushion trucks to provide the utmost in protection from vertical shocks. To call attention to the new car, it was painted beige with red lettering and red doors.

(All: ACL Photo)

Between 1962 and 1964, the ACL ordered almost 800 of the Class O-35 boxcars from Pullman-Standard. These XML 50-foot steel cars had a 9-foot door opening, extended couplers and cushion underframe. They were also equipped with special loading devices that prevented damage to lading and were marked with the letters "DF" to indicate their special purpose. The Class O-35, such as No. 35594, were the state of the art in boxcar construction at that time.

The hand brake end of DF 50-foot Class O-35 boxcar No. 35594.

(ACL Photo)

Class O-38 "DF" 50-foot single door boxcar No. 37322 carries the new "Thanks For Using Coast Line" slogan in this 1964 photograph.

(ACL Photo)

Class O-36-A "DF" single door boxcar No. 15100 was built in 1965 and was photographed at Waycross, Georgia. One of 100 such cars, they were specifically designed for the shipment of gypsum products. The 50-foot 70-ton boxcar had a combination plug-type and sliding door arrangement that provided an opening of 16-feet. Cushion underframes to absorb impacts and special protection against condensation insured against damage to the lading.
(ACL Photo)

ACL Furniture/ Automobile boxcar No. 14199 was built in 1941 by the Mt. Vernon Car Company. Designated as Class O-22, these cars were numbered in the series 14100-14199. The double door cars were of steel construction and had double wood floors. By 1965, only five of the Class O-22 cars remained on the ACL's rolling stock roster.

(ACL Photo)

ACL Stock Car No. 140449 had a capacity of 40 tons, was wooden with steel underframe, and an over-all length of 44 feet. Designated as Class N-5 (number series 140400-140449), the cars were built by the Mt. Vernon Car Company in 1941. They were the last stock cars purchased by the ACL and 23 remained on the rolling stock roster in 1965.

(ACL Photo)

With the development of the paper industry in the South after the First World War, pulpwood became important commodity for the railroads. Hence, the pulpwood car, or wood rack as they were commonly called, was a familiar sight on the many local freight trains that worked the sawmills, lumber yards and team tracks scattered throughout the ACL's system. ACL Pulpwood Car No. 70335 was one of the 150 Class W-5 cars (numbered 70200-70349) that were built by the ACL shop forces in 1951. These cars had a capacity of 50 tons, or 22 cords of wood. Pulpwood Car No. 70335 is stenciled "Assigned to Northern Division."

(All: ACL Photo)

Pulpwood Car No. 71512 is one of the almost 1900 Class W-4 cars owned by the ACL. While the Class W-4 cars in the number series 72000-73199 were built by Pullman-Standard in the early 1950 s, the Class W-4 cars in the number series 71500-71524—such as the 71512—were originally built between 1913-1917 and were rebuilt at the ACL's Waycross shops in 1952. These cars also had a 50-ton, or 22 cord capacity.

Pulpwood was originally cut in 4-foot lengths and was loaded by hand onto both sides of the railroad cars that had sloped bottoms and bulkheads to contain the wood. This fully loaded car is ACL Class W-4-A Pulpwood Car No. 110776. The ACL owned 800 such cars in the number series 110000-110799 that were built by Bethlehem Steel in 1953. The 50-ton cars held 22 cords of wood and were equipped with improved shock cushion type trucks, unit brake beams and snubbers.

Looking down on Pulpwood Car No. 111034, we can see the sloped floor of the car. No. 111034 is one of 799 Class W-6 pulpwood cars (numbered 110900-111699) that were purchased by the ACL from AC&F in 1957. The ACL acquired another 212 Class W-6 pulpwood cars in 1965, the last such cars purchased by the railroad. These cars had a capacity of 70-tons, or 30 cords of wood. The cars rode on Barber trucks and had a one piece cast steel underframe. The bulkheads ends consisted of four post cast steel frame with 1/4" solid steel plate.

ACL's Class P-19 Flat Car was built in 1962 at the Waycross shops. The ACL owned 90 of these 50-ton bulkhead flatcars in the number series 78300-78389 that were specifically built to serve the requirements of the gypsum board industry. The cars were equipped with lading band anchors and one of the end bulkheads contained lockers for packaged parts, with locked doors inside so they could not be opened until the car was unloaded.

(All: ACL Photo)

The ACL developed many special cars to serve the needs of the lumber industry. By modifying both pulpwood flat cars and standard flat cars with lading tie-downs and end bulkheads, the industry could reduce the time needed to load and unload the cars by using fork-lift trucks and was spared the cost of blocking and bracing loads. ACL Flat Car No. 78921 was one such car, with its end bulkheads, fixed floor risers and chain load binders. The end bulkheads allowed for heavy and tight loading, while the chain load binders secured unitized lumber without the use of side stakes.

Gondola Car No. 93319 is one of 194 of the ACL Class K-9 gondolas that were numbered in the series 93200-93399. These cars were built by Bethlehem Steel in 1941 and had a capacity of 50-tons. These steel cars had wooden floors.

(All: ACL Photo)

The Class K-15 all steel car was the standard gondola on the ACL. The ACL owned 793 of these cars (numbered 94600-95399), all built by Pullman-Standard in 1948. K-15 No. 95392 represented the class for this builder's photograph. The 50-ton capacity cars were equipped with snubbers, improved shock cushion type trucks and unit brake beams. These gondolas were used to transport scrap and other heavy loads and were also equipped with lading strap anchors for commodities requiring tie-down.

The phosphate industry was one of the ACL's most important customers and the railroad owned a large fleet of covered hopper cars assigned to phosphate service. Dry rock phosphate was transported by the ACL from the Bone Valley area of Florida to the railroad's own phosphate elevator at Port Tampa in covered hopper cars such as No. 8175. This car was one of the Class U-5 (number series 8175-8474) Phosphate Cars (Dry Rock). The cars numbered 8175-8274 were built by the Chickasaw Shipbuilding & Car Co. in 1923. The cars numbered 8275-8474 were built by the Tennessee Coal, Iron and Railroad Co. in 1925-26. The 8175 was an all steel car with a capacity of 50 tons. This builder's photo shows the operating side of the car with the "Yost" self-sealing discharge doors in the closed position.

This brake wheel end view of Class U-8 Phosphate Car No.
9600 shows the eight loading doors on the roof of the car.
(ACL Photo)

The ACL substantially upgraded its fleet of phosphate rock cars after the Second World War. Many of the more than 1800 cars used in the transportation of phosphate dry rock were acquired after the war. The Class U-8 (number series 9600-9999) were built for the ACL by AC&F in 1951. These 70-ton covered hoppers had eight bottom discharge doors, eight roof loading doors, rode on Barber trucks and were equipped with roller bearings.

(Both: ACL Photo)

In 1957, the Greenville Steel Car Co. built 200 covered hopper dry rock phosphate cars for the ACL. Numbered in the series 1000-10199, they were designated the Class U-10. These cars had a capacity of 70 tons, eight roof loading doors and eight bottom discharge doors. They also rode on Barber trucks and were equipped with roller bearings.

In 1941, the ACL received over 1600 new freight cars as a result of contracts awarded in 1940. Fifteen of these new cars were 70-ton covered hopper cement-phosphate cars such as the 85014. Designated the Class L-1 and numbered in the series 85000-85014, the cars were used to transport cement and wet rock phosphate. The cars were built by the Pullman-Standard Car Manufacturing Co. at Bessemer, Alabama and were delivered to the ACL at Montgomery. Loaded to capacity, they could carry the equivalent of approximately 418 barrels of cement. In comparison, box cars at that time could only haul from 135 to 250 barrels of cement.

(ACL Photo)

The ACL purchased 59 additional covered hopper cement-phosphate cars in 1949 from AC&F. Designated the Class L-3, these cars were numbered in the series 85015-85074. Like the Class L-1, they were 70-ton cars with 8 roof loading hatches and 4 bottom discharge doors. However, the Class L-3 cars came with a "Duryea" underframe, drop side sills, and were the only ACL cars whose side sheets enclosed the area between the bays.

(ACL Photo)

Covered Hopper No. 88904 was one of twenty ACL air-slide style hoppers. Designated Class L-8 and numbered in the series 88900-88919, the cars were built by the General American Transportation Corp. of East Chicago, Indiana between 1962 and 1964.

(All: ACL Photo)

In 1964, the ACL purchased eighty-eight all steel covered hoppers with a capacity of 190,000 pounds. Designated Class L-10 and numbered 89100-89189, they were equipped with 10 roof loading hatches and 6 bottom discharge doors. These cars had the large "ACL" initials on their sides that were standard lettering for freight equipment purchased after 1963.

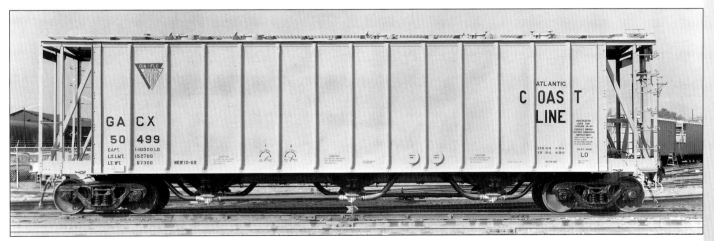

"Dia-Flo" Covered Hopper No. 50499 was one of four GACX cars leased by the ACL from GATX. The car was built by GATX (General American Transportation Corp.) in 1964 and had a capacity of 140,000 pounds.

This overhead view shows the ten roof loading hatches on Class L-14 Covered Hopper No. 120322. This car had a capacity of 200,000 pounds and was purchased by the ACL in 1965.
(ACL Photo)

The "Whopper Hopper" measured 65 feet, 9-1/2 inches over its strikers and its height from rail to top of the side plates was 14 feet, 1-11/16 inches. It was equipped with four hopper compartments with a total of 5,006 cubic feet capacity and its maximum loaded weight was 394,500 pounds. In a single trip, it could transport enough sugar to sweeten 30 million cups of coffee. The car was officially christened at ceremonies in Jacksonville and was then exhibited in major cities in the Southeast for a month. The prototype car was one of a kind as no duplicates were ever built.

(ACL Photo)

Perhaps the most unique unit of ACL's freight equipment was the Class L-12 135-ton Covered Hopper No. 500000—the "Whopper Hopper". Built by Pullman-Standard for the ACL in 1964, it was at that time the largest car of its type in the world and its design included a number of revolutionary features. The car was constructed with Tenelon lightweight stainless steel, developed by U.S. Steel Corp., and possessed a design strength almost twice that of ordinary stainless steel. It was also the first car to use a pair of newly designed six-wheel roller bearing trucks, developed by American Steel Foundries, Inc., which distributed the car's weight evenly over the new type trucks. Another feature unique to covered hoppers was its automatic interior washing system, which is visible in this photo at the end of the car and running along the top.

(ACL Photo)

In addition to its purchase of modern new freight cars, the ACL also remodeled and converted many of its older cars to help meet shipper demands for certain types of special purpose cars. Most of this work was performed at the Waycross car shop. Open-Top Hopper Car No. 83700 began its ACL as one of the 70-ton Class K-16 coal hoppers built for the ACL by the Greenville Steel Car Co. in 1952. When no longer needed for service as a coal hopper car, its sides were raised for service in wood chip service.

(Both: ACL Photo)

Wood chips are produced from debarked slabs and edgings. When pulp and paper mills began to use wood chips in the early-1950s, a new industry was born and the movement of these chips from saw mills to the factories was enormous. It was also a good revenue producer for the ACL. To meet the needs of the industry, the ACL designed and developed its jumbo wood chip car, a 70-ton open top hopper that had double the capacity of earlier wood chip cars. The ACL owned 600 of the Class H-1 Woodchip Hopper Cars, that were built between 1959 and 1964 exclusively for wood chip service. Equipped with snubbers, shock cushion type trucks and unit brake beams, they could be unloaded by existing hopper facilities with either overhead or side type shakers.

ACL No. 80543 is a Class K-3 Coal Dump Car. Built in 1907, this car is shown in a photograph taken at Waycross, Georgia on March 31, 1930. The wooden car had a steel underframe and a capacity of 80,000 pounds.

(Both: ACL Photo)

The ACL Class K-5 steel coal dump cars (number series 81003-81499) were originally between 1921 and 1926 by the Pressed Steel Car Co. and were given heavy repairs at the Waycross shops in 1952. Class K-5 No. 81357 is shown in its original condition at Waycross on March 31, 1930. These cars had latching hopper doors and a capacity of 100,000 pounds.

In 1960, the ACL purchased 200 all steel coal hopper cars with a capacity of 140,000 pounds from the Pullman-Standard Co. Designated as Class K-21, these cars had six bottom discharge doors and were numbered in the series 84000-84199.

(All: ACL Photo)

Top Left: In the early 1950s, the ACL remodeled over 900 of its coal hopper cars to carry wet phosphate rock. The principal change needed for the phosphate service was to increase the angle of the slope sheets so that the cars would be self-emptying. Remodeled Class K-5-B No. 7170 is a former K-5 coal hopper.

Bottom Left: No. 81915 is a 50-ton Class K-8 all steel Coal Hopper Car built for the ACL by Bethlehem Steel Co. in 1940. The K-8 Coal Hoppers (number series 81500-81999) had four bottom Wine Co. discharge doors and rode on either Bettendorf or Buckeye Side Frame type trucks.

ACL Class K-23 Coal Hopper No. 117000 had a capacity of 120,000 pounds and was rebuilt in January of 1967, prior to the ACL merger with the SAL. This four discharge door hopper car was stenciled with the large "ACL" initials that were applied to freight rolling stock after 1963.

The Class M-3 and M-4 cabooses represented the standard design for the ACL's large fleet of wooden cabooses. All of these cabooses were built and/or rebuilt by the ACL at its Waycross shops. Some of the M-3 cabooses were originally built prior to the turn of the century and were rebuilt at Waycross between 1925-1927. Other M-3's were built new at Waycross between 1922-1926. Numbered in the series 01-0459 and 0580-0596, they were traditional red cabooses with centered cupola, four windows on each side and four wheel trucks. M-3 Caboose No. 0447 displays the "Prismo" side and end stripes applied by the ACL from 1951 to 1958.

(ACL Photo)

The Flagman gives the photographer
a friendly wave from M-3 Caboose
No. 085 as his train passes at
Fayetteville, North Carolina.
(ACL Photo)

M-3 Class Caboose No. 0268 sported a "one-of-a-kind" paint scheme. In March of 1962, the caboose was painted white with red lettering, including the "Thanks for Using Coast Line" slogan. The only ACL caboose to receive such treatment, it was assigned to operate on the new piggyback trains and appeared in company publicity photos and the company calendar. The caboose is shown here freshly painted in March of 1962. It would be repainted white again in September of 1963, but probably ended its career on the ACL in the standard caboose car red paint scheme. It was one of the M-3 cabooses equipped with electric lights and radio communication equipment.

(ACL Photo)

In the 1960s, the ACL began to replace its aging fleet of wooden caboose cars with home built steel cabooses. Using components from retired steel boxcars, the Waycross shops built 187 steel cabooses designated as Class M-5 and numbered in the series 0600-0786. The steel cabooses retained the basis appearance of the ACL M-3 and M-4 wooden cabooses with the exception that their four side windows and the cupola were slightly off center. The steel cabooses also sported a new paint scheme consisting of bright orange with black lettering. As shown in this photo of freshly painted M-5 No. 0600, these cabooses also continued to display the company slogan "Thanks for Using Coast Line."

(ACL Photo)

The ACL maintained a fleet of tank cars for use in company service. Tank Car No. 66215 was built in 1912 and is shown in service at Waycross, Georgia on March 31, 1930.

(Both: ACL Photo)

The ACL fueled its diesel locomotives at 33 different locations and a number of the railroad's tank cars were assigned to both store and transport diesel fuel oil to the various fueling facilities. ACL Tank Car No. 66298 was built in 1948 and was one of a number of such cars used in diesel fuel oil service.

The ACL's mechanical department was always innovative when it came to finding new uses for outdated rolling stock. Such innovations included the conversion of several old steam locomotive tenders to cars for the storage of diesel fuel oil. No. 66480 was a former C&WC steam locomotive tender that was converted into a fuel oil storage tank for use at Wilmington, North Carolina.

(Both: ACL Photo)

Another ACL conversion was this use of a former steam locomotive's tender to create a fire fighting equipment car for the terminal at Jacksonville, Florida. The former steam locomotive tender was cut down and attached to the flat car for the storage of water to extinguish fires at remote locations in the yard. The other portion of the car, which appears to be the remains of a locomotive cab, was converted to house a water pump and other fire fighting equipment.

ACL Air Dump Car No. 165274 was used as a ballast car in maintenance of way service. It was built for the ACL by the Magor Car Corporation in 1951 and had a capacity of 30 yards of ballast.

(Both: ACL Photo)

The ACL had a number of wrecking cranes assigned to various locations on its system. This photograph of Wrecking Crane No. 65301 was taken at Waycross, Georgia on March 31, 1930. At that time, No. 65301 was assigned to Waycross and the gentleman posing on the wrecker is its Operator—Hero Zindema—who was about to retire after many years of railroad service. This 160-ton wrecking crane was built in 1925 by Industrial Works and was later assigned to Manchester, Georgia.

BIBLIOGRAPHY

BOOKS:

Beebe, Lucius and Clegg, Charles, *The Trains We Rode, Vol. 1*, Berkeley, California: Howell-North, 1965.

Calloway, Warren L., *Atlantic Coast Line - The Diesel Years*, Halifax, Pennsylvania:Withers Publishing, 1993.

Castner, Charles B., Jr. and Flanary, Ronald C. and Dorin, Patrick C., *Louisville and Nashville Railroad - The Old Reliable* Lynchburg, Virginia: TLC Publishing,1996.

Castner, Charles B. Jr., *Nashville, Chattanooga & St. Louis Railway - The Dixie Line*, Newton, New Jersey: Carstens Publications, Inc., 1995.

Goolsby, C. L., *Atlantic Coast Line Passenger Service: The Postwar Years* Lynchburg, Virginia: TLC Publishing, 1999.

Griffin, William E., Jr., *The Richmond, Fredericksburg and Potomac Railroad: The Capital Cities Route*, Lynchburg, Virginia: TLC Publishing, 1994.

Griffin, William E., Jr., *The Richmond, Fredericksburg and Potomac Railroad Passenger Service - 1935-1975*, Lynchburg, Virginia: TLC Publishing, 2000.

Hoffman, Glen, *Building a Great Railroad: A History of the Atlantic Coast Line Railroad*, ed. Richard E. Bussard, Jacksonville, Florida: CSX Transportation, 1998.

Kratville, William W., *Steam, Steel and Limiteds*, Omaha, Nebraska: William W. Kratville, 1962.

Maiken, Peter T., *Night Trains*, Baltimore, Maryland: The Johns Hopkins University Press, 1992.

Mann, Robert W., *Rails 'Neath the Palms*, Burbank, California: Darwin Publications, 1983.

Prince, Richard E., *Atlantic Coast Line Railroad Steam Locomotives, Ships and History*, Green River, Wyoming: Richard E. Prince, 1966.

Welsh, Joseph M., *By Streamliner: New York to Florida*, Andover, New Jersey: Andover Junction Publications, 1994.

ARTICLES:

"ACL Head End Cars", parts I and II, *Lines South*, June and September, 1985.

"ACL Heavyweight Coaches", parts I and II, *Lines South*, October 1983 and January 1984.

"ACL Pulpwood Cars", *Lines South*, 7:4, Summer 1990.

Eichelberger, George, "ACL W-4 and SAL R-7 Pulpwood Cars", *Lines South*, 5:3, January, 1988.

Eichelberger, George and Goolsby, C. L., "ACL K-7 Low Side Gons", *Lines South*, 7:4, Spring 1990.

Goolsby, C. L., "Atlantic Coast Line Miscellaneous Steel Head End Cars", *Lines South*, September 1986.

Goolsby, C. L., "Atlantic Coast Line Conventional Steel RPO, RPO-Baggage, and Baggage Cars", parts I and II, *Lines South*, 6:3, January, 1989.

Goolsby, C. L., "Atlantic Coast Line Heavyweight Coaches", parts I and II, *Lines South*, 1:2 and 3, October 1983 and January 1984.

Goolsby, C. L., "Atlantic Coast Line Miscellaneous Steel Head End Cars", parts I and II, *Lines South*, 4:2 and 3, September and December 1986.

Goolsby, C. L., "Atlantic Coast Line Wood Cabooses", parts I and II, *Lines South*, 5:2, September 1987 and 9:4, Summer 1992.

Goolsby, C. L., "ACL's Whopper Hopper", *Lines South*, 10:3, Third Quarter, 1993.

Goolsby, C. L., "Atlantic Coast Line R-1 4-8-4s", *Lines South*, 15:3, Third Quarter 1998.

Goolsby, C. L., "ACL and SAL Two-Bay Covered Cement Hoppers", *Lines South,* 15:4, Fourth Quarter, 1998.

"The Modern Atlantic Coast Line", *Modern Railroads*, May, 1954.

Rocky Mount, North Carolina *Telegram*, October 29, 1995.

Savchak, Michael W., "Observation Cars South", *Lines South*, 17:3, Third Quarter, 2000.

Welsh, Joseph, "Lost Elegance; The Florida Special", *Passenger Train Journal*, 22:4, April 1991.

COMPANY PUBLICATIONS AND DOCUMENTS:

Atlantic Coast Line Annual Reports (various years).

Atlantic Coast Line Employee and Public Timetables (various years).

Atlantic Coast Line Freight Schedules (various years).

Atlantic Coast Line News (employee magazine) 1937-1967.

Atlantic Coast Line Pamphlets, Brochures, Correspondence, etc.

Atlantic Cost Line Rosters of Equipment and Equipment Data Books.

In a scene that perfectly captures the nature of the countryside along the ACL's tracks in Virginia and the Carolinas, P-5-B Pacific No. 1650 steams past a tobacco barn south of Ahoskie, North Carolina on June 21, 1949 with a southbound freight train from Portsmouth, Virginia enroute to Rocky Mount, North Carolina. Diesel locomotives were rapidly taking over the main line assignments and in another three years steam would be almost completely gone from the ACL. However, on this glorious summer day in 1949, H. Reid recorded this memorable view of steam in operation during its final days on the ACL.

(H. Reid Photo/Old Dominion Chapter, NRHS Collection)

Top Left: Long after the ACL dieselized its own main line operations, steam locomotives of the Norfolk and Western Railway continued to operate on the ACL main line between Richmond and Petersburg, Virginia. These ACL connection trains carried through Washington-Norfolk coaches and Richmond sleepers for Roanoke and Bristol. Here we see N&W 4-8-2 No. 123 as it crosses the RF&P/ACL bridge over the James River with the southbound Richmond-Petersburg local in the summer of 1956. Notice the "ACL purple" river sign at the far right.

(William B. Gwaltney Photo/Evan D. Siler Collection)

Bottom Left: The ACL first applied its purple, aluminum and yellow paint scheme to E3A passenger diesels in 1939. This paint scheme remained the standard until 1957, when the ACL began to repaint the diesels in a black and yellow scheme. ACL E6A No. 509 still had its purple paint scheme when this photo was taken at the RF&P's Acca Yard in Richmond, Virginia on September 7, 1957. Note that the unit has the painted road numbers that the ACL added to some of its diesels beginning in 1946 and the original ACL medallion with aluminum background and purple lettering.

(Robert S. Crockett Photo)

ATLANTIC
COAST LINE
RAILROAD

In another photo taken at Acca Yard in Richmond on September 7, 1957, ACL E6A No. 513 is shown alongside an RF&P E8A. This ACL E6A exhibits the centered road name lettering and purple medallion background with aluminum lettering that was later added to some of the diesels.

(Robert S. Crockett Photo)

The ACL In Color

When Tom Rice became president of the ACL in 1957, he introduced a new black and yellow paint scheme for the railroad's diesel locomotives. E6A No. 515 sports the black paint scheme at Augusta, Georgia in April of 1967.

(Richard Short Photo/Ray Sturges Collection)

Top Right: In a classic view, ACL dual service cab unit FP7A No. 861 leads E7A and E7B units in the motive power consist of Train No. 375, the southbound *Everglades*, as the train passes by the Seaboard Air Line Railway's Hermitage Yard at Richmond, Virginia in November of 1958. The train had just departed Broad Street Station and is passing under the North Boulevard bridge enroute to the James River Branch. Other items of interest in this photo are the ACL RPO car in the purple paint scheme and the red and black SAL switcher parked by the Seaboard office at Hermitage Yard.

(William B. Gwaltney Photo/
Old Dominion Chapter, NRHS Collection)

Bottom Right: ACL E6A No. 520 is shown with northbound Train No. 376 (the *Everglades*) as it leaves double track and approaches the single track bridge over the Appomattox River at Petersburg, Virginia on the afternoon of August 16, 1963. The ACL train will also pass over the main line of the Seaboard Air Line Railway and the passenger line of the Norfolk and Western Railway as it makes its way to the North Petersburg station at Ettrick, Virginia.

(Ralph Coleman Photo)

ACL Train No. 375, the southbound *Everglades*, is shown on the south leg of the Acca "Y" as the train enters the RF&P's James River Branch on its trip to Petersburg after departing Broad Street Station in the summer of 1956. The train's motive power is provided by E7A No. 524, which was involved in a wreck and retired in 1962. Behind the train are freight cars at the SAL's Hermitage Yard. The tracks above and to the right of the train are industrial tracks worked by the RF&P's yard crews.

(William B. Gwaltney photo/ Old Dominion Chapter, NRHS Collection)

Top Right: ACL F7A No. 366 was one of the railroad's many workhorse freight diesels that toiled on the railroad from 1950 until the merger with the SAL in 1970. It was photographed at Acca Yard in Richmond, Virginia on September 7, 1957.

(Robert S. Crockett Photo)

Bottom Right: The ACL owned a large fleet of general purpose GP-7 diesels that were all acquired between 1950 and 1951. Until 1957, the GP-7 diesels also were painted in the purple, aluminum and yellow paint scheme. This unit has a medallion with aluminum lettering on a purple background. GP-7 No. 200 is at the RF&P's Acca Yard in Richmond, Virginia on October 12, 1958.

(Robert S. Crockett Photo)

In the fall of 1954, ACL GP-7 No. 127 still sports its original paint scheme as it works a local freight in South Richmond, Virginia. This GP-7 has a medallion with purple lettering and an aluminum background.

(William B. Gwaltney Photo/ Old Dominion Chapter, NRHS Collection)

Top Right: ACL GP-7's were also repainted in the new black and yellow paint scheme beginning in 1957. No. 155 is shown with a local freight at Selma, North Carolina on August 9, 1961.

(William B. Gwaltney Photo/ Old Dominion Chapter, NRHS Collection)

Bottom Right: The ACL GP-30's were the railroad's first new motive power delivered in the black and yellow paint scheme. Delivered in January of 1963, they were also the first locomotives purchased by the ACL in more than ten years. Four new GP-30's, led by No. 906, head up a freight train at Rocky Mount, North Carolina in May of 1963.

(William B. Gwaltney Photo/ Old Dominion Chapter, NRHS Collection)

GP-30 No. 906 again heads up a freight train, this time crossing the ACL's single track bridge over the Appomattox River at Petersburg, Virginia on August 16, 1963.

(Ralph Coleman Photo)

The Lummis Peanut Company gives away the location of this photo. We're in Suffolk, Virginia, the "peanut capital of America". The ACL reached Suffolk on its line from Rocky Mount, North Carolina to Portsmouth, Virginia. ACL GP-7 No. 145 and Class M-4 caboose No. 0544 await their next assignment on October 21, 1961.
(William B. Gwaltney Photo/
Old Dominion Chapter, NRHS Collection)

ACL M-3 Class caboose No. 061 is in service at Rocky Mount, North Carolina in December of 1967.
(H. Reid Photo/Old Dominion Chapter, NRHS Collection)

ACL M-3 Class caboose No. 0180 brings up rear of a southbound freight train (behind a Virginian Railway hopper car) as the train passes through Acca Yard in Richmond, Virginia on February 7, 1960.

(Roy Blanchard Photo/
Old Dominion Chapter, NRHS Collection)

ACL Class 0-17 wooden ventilated boxcar awaits its next assignment at St. Paul, North Carolina. This car was built in 1923 and was still in revenue service when photographed on August 9, 1958.

(H. Reid Photo/Old Dominion Chapter, NRHS Collection)

Jarrett, Virginia, located 58 miles south of Richmond, was once a fascinating location for train watching as the east-west main line of the Virginian Railway crossed the ACL's main line racetrack between Richmond and Jacksonville. This photo of the ACL's station at Jarrett was taken on January 23, 1956.
(H. Reid Photo/Old Dominion Chapter, NRHS Collection)

ACL E6A No. 516 and two other E6A units roll Train No. 375, the southbound *Everglades*, through South Richmond, Virginia in December of 1956.
(William B. Gwaltney Photo/ Old Dominion Chapter/NRHS Collection)

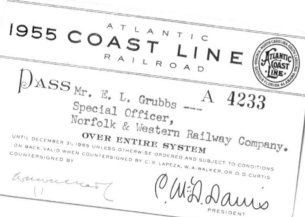

Top: During the Champ Davis era, the ACL made frequent use of the color purple on its motive power, rolling stock and structures. Purple was even used on company publications such as this famous post card of the East and West Coast Champions passing under a palm tree.

(William E. Griffin, Jr. Collection)

Right: The covers of ACL public timetables also made use of the color purple.

(William E. Griffin, Jr. Collection)

Center: Even the Annual Passes bearing Davis' signature were in purple!

(K. L. Miller Collection)

Luncheon Menu

ATLANTIC COAST LINE RAILROAD

SOUPS AND APPETIZERS

Consomme, Hot or Jellied .40
Chilled Fruit or Vegetable Juice .25
Hearts of Florida Celery .40

Fruit Cocktail .65
Spanish Bean Soup .40
Olives .40

Cream of Tomato Soup .40
Large Glass Florida Orange Juice .40
Celery and Olives .40

SUGGESTIONS

Veal and Ham Pie, en casserole Served with Whipped Potatoes, Turnip Greens
Bread and Beverage
2.40

Bacon, Lettuce and Tomato Sandwich, Served with Beverage and Choice of Dessert 1.75
Cold Salmon, Tartar Sauce, Potato Salad, Tomato Slices 1.85
Three Decker Club Sandwich (Turkey) Served with Cup of Soup and your choice of Beverage 2.15
Bacon (3 strips) or Sugar Cured Ham with Eggs, French Fried Potatoes, Toast or Bread, Beverage 2.00
Turkey Salad, Served with Saltines, Beverage and Dessert 2.15
Welsh Rarebit, Chef's Salad, Dry Toast, Choice of Beverage 1.75
Vegetable Plate, Poached Egg, Bread and Butter, Choice of Beverage 1.85
Toasted Turkey Sandwich, Fruit Salad, Beverage and Dessert 1.85
Sardines in Oil, Potato Salad, Tomato Slices, Served with Saltines and Choice of Beverage 2.00
Cup of Soup, Bowl of Chili Con Carne, Mixed Salad, Saltines, Beverage 1.80
Fried Fillet of Fish, Tartar Sauce, Potatoes, Bread, Beverage 2.20

Turkey a la king, Served with Whipped Potatoes,
Turnip Greens, Bread and Beverage
2.40

BREADS ETC.

Assorted Bread .25
Milk Toast .65

Toast .25

Crackers .10
Cream Toast .85

DESSERTS

Ice Cream, with Wafers .35
Camembert, Swiss Gruyere or Blue Cheese, Crackers .45

Stewed Prunes in Syrup .40
Jello with Mixed Fruit .35

Chilled Melon .50

BEVERAGES

Coffee, Postum, Cocoa, Sanka, Tea .35

Milk, Buttermilk .30

For Children •

Parents may share their portions with children without extra charge.
One egg with two vegetables, bread and butter, a glass of milk and ice cream
1.30

An extra charge of 50 cents per person will be made for meals served out of dining car.
The States of Pennsylvania and Florida assess a Sales Tax of three per cent which must be collected from the buyer.
Patrons are respectfully requested to write their orders on meal checks and pay only on presentation of such checks.
Waiters are forbidden to accept verbal orders.
Suggestions for the betterment of the service are invited.
J. B. MASHBURN, Supt. Dining Cars
Atlantic Coast Line R. R. Co., Washington, D. C.

This young couple is about to enjoy and steak and home fries dinner aboard one of the ACL dining cars.

(ACL Photo)

Of course, the menus also featured the purple ink as well. Interestingly enough, the china did not include purple, but a grey band.

(K.L. Miller Collection)

The ACL In Color

Uniformed hostesses led passengers in games, sing-alongs and fashion shows onboard the *Florida Special's* twin unit dining cars that were refurbished to serve as recreation cars. This photo shows the interior of the *Winter Haven*.

(ACL Photo)

The ACL disappeared officially on July 1, 1967, but one last passenger timetable was issued depicting the two merged roads heralds. Of course, the purple color, long prevalent, has disappeared in favor of the SAL orange.

(K. L. Miller Collection)

PASSENGER SCHEDULES
Effective July 1, 1967